The TEEN RELATIONSHIP Workbook:

for professionals helping teens to develop healthy relationships and prevent domestic violence

68 reproducible worksheets about...

- Evaluating Your Relationships
- Understanding Abuse
- Social Influences
- Building Healthy Relationships
- Making Good Decisions

by Kerry Moles, CSW

Illustrated by Amy Leutenberg Brodsky, LISW

© 2001 WELLNESS Reproductions and Publishing, LLC 1-800 / 669-9208

ACKNOWLEDGEMENTS

"When you learn, teach. When you get, give." – Maya Angelou

My thanks to all of the people who have given me the professional knowledge about domestic violence, teen relationship abuse and youth work that has contributed to this book: The staff and volunteers of the Pasadena YWCA Rape Crisis Center volunteer class of 1991; Melinda Kaiser, formerly of My Sister's Place; JCCA's Independent Living team and their youth development consultant Joan Morse, who taught me the value of 'portfolios'; Barbara Wachtel from the Pleasantville Diagnostic Center; the entire central office staff at the Center for the Elimination of Violence in the Family; Carol Morrison and all of the staff and co-instructors in the Safe Horizons Alternatives to Violence Program; and the members of the Teen Abuse Forum. I am especially grateful to Karen Wilson and Barri Rosenbluth from SafePlace (formerly the Austin Center for Battered Women.) My work in this field has grown out of my short but rich experience as a volunteer under their direction in CBW's Teen Dating Violence Project.

I am so appreciative of Kathy, Estelle and everyone at Wellness Reproductions and Publishing for their boundless enthusiasm, encouragement and personal attention during our partnership in developing this book. Estelle's contagious energy made it possible for me to finish this book when I was feeling overworked, overwhelmed and over-pregnant. Amy Leutenberg Brodsky combined her talent as an artist and a social worker to create unique illustrations for every activity that reflect and complement the emotional content of this book. Thanks also to Jay Leutenberg for printing the book with T.L.C., the book's Graphic Computer Artist Joan Allison, Product Administrator Lucy Ritzic, and to Bob Neillie, for his proofreading and encouraging notes.

My gratitude to Mark Constantine for his legal assistance; Winslow for help with resources in the U.K.; Source RE Source for help with resources in Canada; and Sandra Negley, author of *Crossing the Bridge*, for her valuable input.

On a personal note, I thank my husband Eric Nicklas for his faith, support and encouragement as I have worked on this book and in every other aspect of our lives. I can't imagine a greater life's partner or a better parent and role model for our new son. And lastly, I owe everything to my own 'relationship role models', my parents Pat and Bill Moles. In 42 years of marriage, they have raised my sisters Karen and Kim and brother Michael and I with unconditional love and support, and shown us that relationships are partnerships and all people are of equal value and potential.

This book is dedicated to the many young people I have worked with over the years who have let me into their lives, trusted me with their stories, and inspired me with their strength and resilience. I am particularly thankful to the members of the Pleasantville Cottage School's Youth Leadership Program, the '97-'98 Youth Council of the Community Opportunity Center of the Tarrytowns, and the youth leaders of Roosevelt High School's Relationship Abuse Prevention Program. They have taught me more than I could ever hope to teach them.

TABLE OF CONTENTS

Foreword	i
Using *The Teen Relationship Workbook*	ii
Portfolio Cover Sheet	iii
A Message To Teens from the Author	iv
Tips for Facilitators	
How to Help Victims of Teen Relationship Abuse	v
Working with Abusive Teens	vi
Tips for Parents	vii

SECTION	ACTIVITY	PAGE
EVALUATING YOUR RELATIONSHIP		
	My Support Map *	1
	Evaluating My Relationship	3
	How Healthy is My Relationship? *	5
	Quiz: What Would You Do…?	7
	Different Types of Relationships	10
	3 Kinds of Love	12
	How My Relationship Affects My Life	16
	Balancing You, Me and Us	19
UNDERSTANDING ABUSE		
	Myths & Facts on Domestic Violence & Teen Relationship Abuse	21
	Understanding Power and Control	24
	Understanding Equality	27
	Focus on Emotional Abuse	30
	Case Study: Emotional Abuse	32
	Focus on Physical Abuse	34
	Focus on Sexual Abuse	36
	Painful Memory	38
	Focus on Sexual Harassment	40
	The Cycle of Abuse	43
	21 Warning Signs of an Abusive Person	45
	Why People Stay In Abusive Relationships	47
SOCIAL INFLUENCES		
	Gender Roles: Men & Women *	50
	Gender Roles: Where Do I Stand?	52
	The Gender Roles Around Us	54
	My Relationship Role Models	56
	Choosing My Relationship Values	59
	What's Age Got to Do With It?	61
	Violence at Home	63

SECTION	ACTIVITY	PAGE

BUILDING HEALTHY RELATIONSHIPS

    The Do's and Don'ts of Starting a Relationship — 65
    What to Look for in a Partner * — 67
    Understanding Boundaries * — 69
    Practicing Boundary Setting — 72
    How Do You Relate? — 74
    Assert Yourself With "I" Statements — 76
    Building Self-Esteem through Positive Self-Talk — 78
    Action Plan for Improving My Self-Esteem * — 80
    Let's Talk about Sex — 83
    The Relationship Bill of Rights — 86

MAKING GOOD DECISIONS

    Contract with Myself — 88
    Should I Stay or Should I Go? — 90
    Goals for Improving My Relationship — 92
    Ending a Relationship — 95
    Dealing with a Breakup — 97
    Safety Plan — 100
    Orders of Protection — 105
    Is My Relationship Ready for a Baby? Am I? — 107
    For My Partner & Me: Decisions About Having a Baby — 110
    The Effects of Relationship Abuse on Children — 112
    Acquaintance Rape: What You Can Do to Avoid It! — 114
    How to Help a Friend — 116

REVIEW

    Relationship Crossword Puzzle — 118

RESOURCE SECTION

    Where to Get Help and Information on Domestic Violence and Relationship Abuse — a
    Additional Resources: Recommended Readings and Videos — b
    References — c

* Presentation Posters available

FOREWORD

The TEEN RELATIONSHIP Workbook is for the therapist, counselor, group facilitator or other helping professional working with young people to prevent or end relationship abuse. This workbook can be used in individual counseling sessions, educational settings and psycho-educational or support groups.

Teaching teens to recognize the warning signs of relationship abuse and develop skills for healthy relationships can help to stop the cycle of violence that in so many ways threatens the physical and emotional health of today's young people, tomorrow's adults and our society in general. Although this workbook is certainly appropriate as a means of general education on relationship issues, it is primarily intended as a tool for engaging victims, perpetrators and those at risk of being either, in the following tasks:

1. Identifying the healthy and unhealthy characteristics of relationships they are in, have been in or may be in, in the future;
2. Understanding the dynamics of emotional, physical and sexual abuse in intimate relationships;
3. Exploring and clarifying their own values, beliefs and attitudes about gender roles and intimate relationships;
4. Becoming empowered to make positive, healthy decisions about their own intimate relationships.

Teen relationship abuse, also called 'teen dating violence' or 'domestic violence among teens' is increasingly understood to be as pervasive a problem in today's society as adult domestic violence. Studies show that anywhere between 10% to 63% of teens experience violence in a dating relationship.[1] One in four women will be abused by a partner at some point in her life,[2] and many adult survivors of domestic violence have said that their patterns of abusive relationships began when they were teenagers.

We also know that the prevalence of relationship abuse crosses all lines of race, ethnicity, culture, age, religion, economic status, geography and sexual orientation. Relationship abuse, in its many forms, can happen to ANYONE. For this reason, we have made efforts to use language and artwork that is as inclusive as possible throughout this book. Although using both male and female pronouns in every sentence can make reading more difficult, it is important to remain gender-neutral so that male and female victims and perpetrators, including youth who are gay, lesbian, bisexual or transgender, can relate to the worksheets. We have also tried to be inclusive of the broad range of professionals who work with youth in different settings and capacities. The term 'facilitator' is used to refer to the professional who is guiding this work, whether he or she is a group leader, clinical therapist, youth worker, teacher or other helping adult.

The term 'relationship abuse' is used throughout this book in place of the terms 'domestic violence' or 'teen dating violence' for several reasons. The word 'domestic' implies that the relationship is taking place within the context of marriage or cohabitation, which isn't usually the case with teens. The word 'dating' is not a word that many young people use today (although when we adults use it teens usually know what we're talking about, so it is, for lack of a better term, used occasionally in this book.) Finally, the word 'abuse' is used instead of 'violence' because abuse encompasses a much broader range of behavior than physical violence. Violence is only the tip of the iceberg when it comes to abusive relationships. The hope is that professionals, with the assisstance of this workbook, can help young people to identify the more subtle forms of emotional, verbal, and financial abuse in order to prevent escalation to physical and sexual violence.

USING *The TEEN RELATIONSHIP Workbook*

Who Should Use This Book?

The TEEN RELATIONSHIP Workbook can be used by social workers, psychologists, occupational therapists, youth workers, health care providers, teachers, counselors, or any other professional interested in helping young people to develop healthy relationships. However, it is important that professionals who are not specially trained in issues of domestic violence be aware of the specific and complicated dynamics involved in working with people in abusive relationships. Often, well-meaning and even highly trained mental health professionals can make an abusive situation worse by misinterpreting a person's motives, unintentionally colluding with abusers because they are not aware of the abuser's tactics, or engaging in victim-blaming because they are susceptible to commonly accepted myths and stereotypes about victims of abuse. The supplemental pages of this book include 'tips' for working with teens around issues of relationship abuse. However it is highly recommended that a professional who is not specially trained in this area make use of the recommended reading list, take advantage of opportunities for professional training in domestic violence and relationship abuse, and consult with a domestic violence services agency before beginning your individual or group work in this area.

The Workbook Format

Unlike traditional workbooks, *The TEEN RELATIONSHIP Workbook* is designed in a spiral-bound, easily reproducible format. There are fifty 'activities,' in six sections of the book. Each activity includes one or more worksheets to be photocopied and given to the teen participant, as well as a 'Facilitator's Information' page with suggestions for using the worksheet(s) in group or individual settings. Facilitators can choose which activities to use based on the presenting issues and goals of the group or individual, and in response to the content of previous sessions. The facilitator is essentially able to customize a curriculum for each group or individual.

The interactive and concrete nature of this workbook is especially effective with teens because of the developmental tasks with which they are struggling. The critical task of adolescence, the formation of the sense of identity, is greatly influenced by family and peer relationships but often takes place on a largely subconscious level. Many teens who have witnessed unhealthy relationships begin to perpetuate those unhealthy patterns during adolescence without even realizing it. The activities in this workbook are designed to empower teens to interrupt any unhealthy functioning in relationships, and to base future relationships on a healthier and consciously developing sense of self.

This book's activities allow teens to examine relationship issues in a non-threatening way because many of them do not require the participant to personalize the information. The facilitator can, when teens are ready, introduce activities that challenge them to bring to the forefront their experiences with past relationships, and make concrete decisions about what they want future relationships to look like. The workbook encourages teens to think critically about the influence of social forces and to develop their own system of relationship values.

Facilitators who want to offer teens a more in-depth focus on a particular topic can refer to the follow-up activities and suggestions for pages from other books by Wellness Reproductions and Publishing, Inc. to use in conjunction with that activity.

USING *The TEEN RELATIONSHIP Workbook* (continued)

The Relationship Portfolio

It is recommended that every teen working on material from this book be helped by the facilitator to develop a 'Relationship Portfolio.' Rather than throwing away a completed worksheet or stuffing it in a backpack, the 'portfolio' is a safe place for each teen to collect his or her work. At the beginning of the group or individual work, the facilitator should provide each teen with an empty portfolio, preferably a three-ring binder, although a folder will also do in a crunch. The binders with the clear plastic pockets on the front allow teens to personalize the cover. Following this page, you will find a sample 'cover page' that can be photocopied for teens to decorate and paste on a photo of themselves. You will also find a "message to teens from the author," which may help to explain the purpose of this work.

As the teen completes worksheets during each session and places them in the binder, the binder becomes the teen's own personal 'Relationship Portfolio.' Aside from the work they have done from this book, teens may add anything else they wish to include, such as drawings, letters, pictures, poems or information collected about community resources. The facilitator may want to have on hand a package of clear plastic page protectors, available at most office supply stores, which fit into three-ring binders. Teens can use these to hold pictures and other objects that they can't or don't want to hole-punch.

The portfolio serves several purposes aside from being a place to keep worksheets. It allows teens to have a constant and tangible object from one session to the next. It becomes a reflection of themselves, their thoughts and their work, which they can build and develop and be proud of. It will help in the teen's development of his or her self-concept as a competent person, separate and independent from his or her partner, parents and peer group. Upon termination of the group or indvidual work, the teen can take the portfolio with him or her. It will not only serve as a transitional object but as a practical resource for him or her to refer to when in need of information or a reaffirmation of the decisions made, strengths and values developed, or beliefs defined during the course of this work.

For therapists working with victims or perpetrators of relationship abuse, the portfolio can aid in the clinical work. One of the goals of therapy with many victims and perpetrators is to integrate the split between the 'bad object' and 'good object' or the alternate rage toward and idealization of the partner. The portfolio can facilitate this work because it holds the client's own perceptions from one session to the next. When the client reviews his or her work from the previous sessions, the portfolio provides a window into the split-off perceptions and allows a gentle '*in*' for the therapist to help the client work toward integration.

It should be clear that the portfolio belongs to the teen and will eventually go home with the teen, but it is recommended that the teen leave the portfolio with the facilitator between sessions. This is so the portfolio can be kept in a safe place, won't get lost, and will be sure to be available for every session. The facilitator can make copies of any worksheets the teen wants to bring with him or her. However, if a teen insists on bringing the portfolio with him or her, the facilitator should make and keep copies of everything that goes into the portfolio in case the portfolio is lost or the teen forgets to bring it to a session.

My Relationship Portfolio

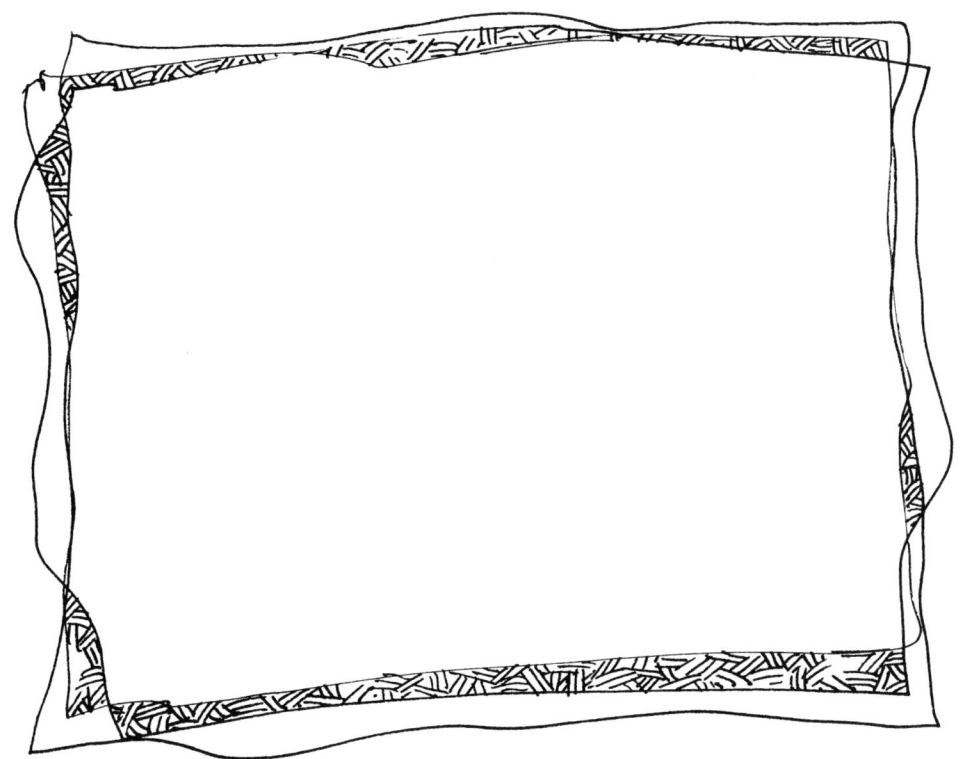

A MESSAGE TO TEENS FROM THE AUTHOR

When I was a teenager dealing with friendships and my first experiences with dating, my mother told me something that stuck with me. She said, "Relationships are the hardest things you'll ever do."

I know now what my mother meant. Every area of everyone's life is filled with relationships: relationships with parents and children, brothers and sisters, with teachers and classmates, co-workers and bosses, with friends and acquaintances and even the guy on the check-out line at the grocery store. All of those relationships are important, and most of them require work. But often the relationships we struggle with most are the relationships with what I call 'intimate partners' – boyfriends, girlfriends, husbands, wives, exes, crushes – anyone you have romantic feelings about.

This book is mostly about that last kind of relationship. Intimate relationships are a challenge for everyone. Learning how relationships 'work' is a lifelong process, just like learning about yourself. People are always changing and growing, and so are the relationships between them. Even when a relationship ends, it may continue to affect you and shape who you are as a person.

Whether you are in a relationship now that you're having difficulty with, have been hurt in the past, have seen bad relationships in your family, or just want to learn about how to have healthy relationships in the future, *The TEEN RELATIONSHIP Workbook* is for you. It will not give you a formula for the perfect relationship – there's no such thing. What it will do is teach you some things we do know about healthy and unhealthy relationships. You will learn about what abuse is and how to avoid it, and what respect is and how to give it and get it. You will evaluate your current or past relationships to figure out what is good or bad about them. You will also explore yourself: what you learned about relationships as a kid, what is most important for you to have in a relationship in the future. You will learn about some of the really sticky situations in relationships, like sexual harassment and even date rape. You will teach yourself about who you are and make decisions about who you want to be.

A counselor, therapist or other adult who wants you to learn to develop healthy relationships will be helping you to put together your own personal book, called your 'Relationship Portfolio,' from some of the activities in this book. They will work with you on completing the worksheets, and help you deal with some of the strong feelings that might come up as you go along. If you are working as part of a group, you will get support from the other group members and will be able to give them support, too.

I hope this workbook will help you begin to build the foundation for a lifetime of healthy relationships.

Sincerely,

Kerry Moles

Kerry Moles
Author, *The TEEN RELATIONSHIP Workbook*

TIPS FOR FACILITATORS:
Working with Teens in Abusive Relationships

How to Help Victims of Teen Relationship Abuse

When working with teens who are being abused, it is often difficult for adults to resist the temptation to immediately rush in and 'save' the victim. Of course, we must intervene whenever anyone is in immediate physical danger, but we should remember that there are very complicated dynamics involved in abusive relationships. Even if we could whisk people away from abusive situations and make sure they never had contact with their abuser again (which we usually can't), there's a lot more involved in helping people change the way they think about relationships and themselves. If this process doesn't take place, it's more likely that the pattern of abusive relationships will repeat itself. Following are some tips to keep in mind when working with teens who may be victims of relationship abuse.

- Show concern - but don't be confrontational. Say "I'm worried that you could get hurt and I want to help," rather than "I know you're getting beat up and you have to break up with the jerk!" People who are being abused are often scared, embarrassed, and unsure about who they can trust. Even when teens deny the violence at first, be patient. Give them some information about relationship abuse, and continue to express interest. Gentle reminders that you are concerned are more likely to make them feel comfortable confiding in you than forceful confrontations, which might alienate teens and scare them off.

- Offer help - but do not insist on taking control. Remember, control is the bottom line in an abusive relationship, and controlling the teen is exactly what the abuser has been trying to do. The objective should be to help the teen take back control him or herself, not to transfer control from the abuser to you. As much as you may believe you know what the right thing is for the teen to do, the decision to leave must be his or her own.

- Be honest. Discuss the limits of confidentiality with teens up front so they know under exactly what conditions you will involve other people including parents, agency or school administrators, and police. If you are afraid that your obligation to report will keep teens from seeking your help, then help them to come up with other people they can talk to or at the very least, suggest they call a confidential hotline.

- If you don't know who the teen's partner is, don't make assumptions about sexual orientation. Use gender-neutral language until the teen has let you know whether his or her partner is male or female.

- Make a safety plan. If there has ever been physical violence, even if teens insist they are not in serious danger, work with them to complete the safety plan in this book to make sure they know what to do if things get violent again.

- Don't ask blaming questions. Don't say things like "What did you do to make him hit you?" or "Why don't you break up with her?" Don't make teens feel like you think they're stupid for staying with their abusers, because you will risk wounding their self-esteem even more and reinforce what their abusers are probably already telling them.

- Don't put down the abuser. Talk about the abusive behavior being unacceptable, but don't 'trash' a person's partner if you want that person to trust you. Whatever you might think of the abuser, the teen may still love this person and probably sees many positive qualities in him or her. Abuse victims will often 'split' their feelings and express rage at their partner one day and act like the relationship is perfect the next day. This is a defense mechanism, and should be treated gently. Try to help the victim integrate the conflicted feelings by acknowledging that both the good and the bad exist in the same person.

How to Help Victims of Teen Relationship Abuse (continued)

- Let teens know you will be supportive whether they stay with their abusers or not. Chances are, the abuser has already begun to isolate the teen from members of his or her support system. If teens think you will abandon them if they don't do what you want them to do, then the abuser's claim that "I'm the only one who's really here for you" is reinforced. If teens know you will stick around, then when they are ready to think about leaving, they will be more likely to seek your help.

- Ask teens how they feel - don't tell them how they feel! Don't say "You don't love him" or "He doesn't love you." Telling teens how they think or feel is one of the quickest ways for adults to alienate them. Instead, take all of their feelings seriously, and acknowledge that it's okay to have conflicting feelings at the same time.

- Keep your own issues in check. Be aware of your 'emotional baggage,' and don't impose it on the teens you are working with. As much as you wish they could learn from your experiences, they can't always.

- Be sensitive to cultural differences. Different cultures have different norms and values regarding the relationships between the sexes, including attitudes toward male domination, violence, sexuality and marriage. The teens you are working with don't have to share your values, but you can help them explore where their values and beliefs come from, and make conscious decisions about the ones that are important to them. Don't be afraid to ask questions about the teen's culture and family belief systems, and work with him or her within that context.

- Figure out what needs are being met by this relationship. If a person chooses to stay in an abusive relationship, it is because they are getting some kind of needs met. They may be emotional, financial, physical, and very likely when it comes to adolescents, social needs like the need for belonging. Your task is to figure out what those needs are, and help the teen develop healthier ways of meeting them. Remember that you may not think certain needs are important, but then you are not a teen - it might help to brush up on your theory of adolescent development.

- Educate. Give teens the facts about teen dating violence. Give them literature like pamphlets from domestic violence organizations and worksheets from this book. This will help them understand they are not alone, and that you are not just making this stuff up. Give teens hotline numbers and tell them they can call anytime, confidentially and for free, to talk to people who deal with this kind of situation all the time. This will give the teen a sense of control.

- If the teen breaks up with the abuser, don't get too invested in the idea that the relationship is over. It's common for victims to leave and go back a number of times before ending the relationship for good. You don't want the teen to be afraid to tell you if she or he reconciles with the abuser.

- If the teen talks to you about the abuse in front of a friend, engage the friend. Teach him or her how to be supportive and how not to blame the victim, and encourage the victim to include the friend in safety planning.

- Encourage involvement of parents, foster parents or caretakers. When teens do not want caretakers involved, explore the reasons, and try to respect them. While you may need to notify a guardian if a teen's life is in danger or depending on your organization's policies, don't assume that all parents will do the best thing for their teen and try to rule out the possibility of the parent being a batterer too. If you do involve caretakers, give them the "Tips for Parents" handout in this book and discuss those suggestions with them

- Get help for yourself. Call a domestic violence agency for guidance. By talking to an expert about the specifics of the situation, you'll be able to gain a better understanding of what you can do that will be most helpful.

TIPS FOR FACILITATORS:
Working with Teens in Abusive Relationships (continued)

Working with Abusive Teens

There is a great deal of controversy among professionals in the field of domestic violence about working with abusers. Advocates for victims are concerned about therapists and programs that treat domestic violence as a 'mental health' issue or an 'anger management' issue, and may fail to hold perpetrators accountable by giving them the message that they can't control their behavior. Some people feel that batterer's intervention programs steal precious resources from programs that serve victims. Experts want to be sure that people working with abusers do not only address physical violence, but also other equally harmful and controlling behaviors such as emotional and financial abuse.

It is the author's opinion that batterer's intervention is a critical part of our society's response to relationship abuse. While it is important to work with everyone affected by abuse, we can not ignore the source of the problem. The emphasis should be on holding the abuser accountable for his or her behavior and educating him or her about the dynamics of all forms of abuse. It is true that recidivism rates, while hard to measure, are extremely high even for perpetrators who have completed batterer's intervention programs. However this does not mean that intervention can not be effective in reducing or ending abusive behaviors in many people - especially early intervention with young people who are not yet as set in their ways as adults. This workbook is intended to be a tool for educating abusive or potentially abusive teens about the dynamics of abuse, and engaging them in the process of changing abusive attitudes, beliefs and values.

With this said, working with abusive teens is usually even more difficult than working with victims. Abusers are much less likely to seek or accept help and often deny the abuse or project blame onto their victims and other people. Abusers are often extremely manipulative - it is easy for service providers to be fooled because they can present as very charming and 'together'! Following are some suggestions for working with teens who are or may be abusive to their intimate partners.

- If you suspect a teen is abusive, confront him or her directly but in a neutral tone of voice. Ask about specific violent behaviors, such as hitting, pushing, and grabbing, rather than talking in general terms like 'fighting.' Also ask about other forms of controlling behavior, such as threats and put-downs. It is important that you identify abusive behaviors without appearing too judgmental. You want to convey the message that you are accepting of the teen, but not accepting of abusive behaviors.

- Be clear about your policy regarding confidentiality, and the situations in which you will have to involve others including parents, school or agency administrators, and police. If you have reason to believe there is a threat of imminent danger, you must notify the police, potential victim and parents of victim and perpetrator.

- Support the teen for talking about the abuse. Acknowledge that it takes courage to admit to problems and to seek help.

- Educate the teen about the different types of abuse, the cycle of abuse and the dynamics of power and control vs. equality. Explore the teen's need to gain power and control over his or her partner.

- Be clear that violence is always a choice. Violence does not happen because a person is provoked, can't handle anger, is drunk or 'out of control.' Violence happens because one person makes a choice to use force to gain power and control over another.

Working with Abusive Teens (continued)

- Do not call relationship abuse an 'anger management' problem. We know that most abusers can control their anger because they do control their anger with people other than their intimate partners and children.

- When the teen talks about anger, acknowledge that angry feelings are acceptable but violence is not. Anger is usually a defense against vulnerability to underlying feelings such as hurt, fear, shame, etc. Help the teen to identify and appropriately express these feelings.

- Constantly be aware of an abuser's tendency to use minimization, denial and blame. Call the abuser on these tactics every time.

- Be careful about the scenario of "we both abuse each other." This is often an attempt to project blame onto the victim, which the victim may believe. While both people may engage in violent behavior or individual acts of abuse, there is usually a pattern of one person controlling the other. The person in control is the abuser. The other person may simply be fighting back in an attempt to regain control of his or her own life.

- Explore where the teen learned to link violence with intimate relationships. More often than not, an abusive person experienced or witnessed abuse at home. Everyone gets messages promoting sexism and violence from many aspects of society. No matter where they learned the violence, they have the ability to make their own choices about whether to use it in their own relationships.

- Help the teen to identify the current and potential consequences of the abuse - how it affects the partner and the relationship, as well as school, family, friends, and feelings about self. Explore possible future consequences including jail, an escalating, life-long pattern of abusive relationships, and a cycle of violence that extends to the teen's own children.

- Help the teen to reduce objectification and develop empathy for his or her partner and other potential victims.

- NEVER engage in 'couples counseling' with abusers and victims. This is a set-up for the victim, who will not be able to talk openly in front of the abuser anyway.

- NEVER tell an abuser anything his or her partner has told you, even if you think what you are saying is harmless.

- Encourage involvement of parents, foster parents or caretakers, but allow teen to make this decision unless there is imminent danger. When involving caretakers, remember that an abusive teen is more likely to come from an abusive home environment.

- Don't think one good talk will change the abuse. It takes a lot to change a lifetime of abusive attitudes, beliefs and behaviors. Change is not likely to take place without ongoing education, long-term counseling that holds the abuser accountable for his or her behavior, and most importantly, the abuser has to make a choice to change.

- Get help for yourself. Seek the advice of a domestic violence agency that works with batterers or a carefully screened batterer's intervention program, and take advantage of the suggested readings on working with abusers.

TIPS FOR PARENTS:
When your teen is being hurt by a boyfriend or girlfriend

- Listen and don't judge. Don't punish. If your teen believes s/he will be listened to and not yelled at or given ultimatums, s/he will be more likely to be honest with you and let you help.

- Don't blame your teen. Violence is always the choice of the abuser, but the abuser may have your teen convinced s/he 'brings it on' or does something to deserve it. Let your child know s/he does not deserve to be abused. Don't ask blaming questions like "What did you do to make him hit you?" or "Why do you let this happen?"

- Don't put your teen down. S/he has been put down enough by the abuser. Don't give your teen the message that you think s/he is stupid or senseless for being in this relationship. Instead, talk about your child's strengths and focus on positive behavior.

- Take your teen's feelings seriously. Remember your first love? Could anyone have told you it wasn't really love? Acknowledge that your teen's feelings about his/her partner, both the good and the bad, are real. Don't tell your teen s/he doesn't love the partner or expect your teen to just 'get over' the partner, because it's not that simple. It is possible to love someone who hurts you.

- Don't get into a power struggle by forbidding your teen to see the partner. If you do this, your teen will probably go behind your back, and then s/he will not be able to come to you when s/he really needs help! You will also set yourself up as the 'bad guy' and play right into the abuser's hands by making it seem like you are the enemy and the abuser is the good one. If you can offer patient support, your teen will be much more likely to come to the decision to end the relationship on his/her own, and learn how to have healthier relationships in the future.

- Help your teen plan a safe way to see his/her partner. For example, allow them to spend private time together in your home, where you are within ear shot but not in the room. Help develop a safety plan so s/he knows what to do under different circumstances if it gets violent. Tell your teen you will pick her/him up any time, anywhere s/he feels unsafe, without punishing.

- Allow your teen as much control as possible. Empower your teen to make healthy decisions. Obviously safety is your first priority, but it is important to allow your teen to make his/her own decisions whenever it is safe to do so. The abuser has taken away your teen's power and control, and if you do the same, it may make matters worse.

- Reassure your teen of your love and concern, and your wish to help do what's best for him or her.

- Call a domestic violence agency or hotline. You can get information about relationship abuse, advice on how to help your child, and support for yourself to deal with your own anger and frustration. The National Domestic Violence Hotline is 1-800-799-SAFE. They can give you referrals for agencies in your area.

- Get your teen into counseling, preferably with an agency or counselor who specializes in domestic violence and teen relationship abuse. Even if s/he ends the relationship, it will take time and work to repair the emotional damage that has been done by the abuse. Counseling will also help your teen learn how to avoid abusive relationships in the future.

- Do not threaten violence against the abuser. This just reinforces the idea that problems can be solved with violence. If it's okay for you, then it's okay for them. Instead, let your teen and his/her partner know that you will call the police if you ever witness violence.

- If the abuser goes to the same school, help your teen figure out who at the school s/he can talk to and make a part of the safety plan.

- If your teen breaks up with the abuser, be aware that the break-up period is the most dangerous time. Ask your local domestic violence agency about how to get an order of protection.

My Support Map

Although you may be thinking a lot about your relationships with 'romantic' or 'intimate' partners, first let's take a look at some of the other relationships in your life. This is important, because sometimes we focus so intensely on one relationship that we lose sight of the importance of our other relationships, like with friends, family and other people who can help us reach our goals. Remember that no one relationship can ever meet all of your needs.

Below you can create a 'map' of your support system. In the center circle, put your name or paste a picture of yourself. In the boxes connected to you, write the names and telephone numbers of the people or organizations who are or could be a part of your support system. This means anyone you could call on for help or support in any area of your life from a serious personal problem, to health care, to help with your math homework. Feel free to draw in extra boxes if necessary!

Examples of people and places you might have in your support system . . .

- Parents
- Brothers or sisters
- Other family members
- Close friends
- A teacher you trust
- Your counselor or therapist
- Your church, temple or place of worship
- Your dating partner
- Youth center
- Crisis hotline or youth line
- Health clinic
- A club, team or group you belong to
- Your co-workers or boss
- Your school
- Other _____
- Other _____

As you continue to work on developing healthy relationships, strong or confusing feelings may come up. Who in your support system can you talk with about these feelings?

Facilitator's Information for
My Support Map

Purpose: To identify supportive people and organizations where teens can seek help with relationships and other issues.

Materials: One photocopy of worksheet per participant
Instant camera or existing picture of each teen
Glue stick or rubber cement
Fine-tipped colored markers
Phone book
List of numbers for local/state hotlines, shelters, youth counseling centers, etc.
Optional: Flipchart and markers/blackboard and chalk

Activity (Group or Individual):
1. Explain to participant(s) that they will be creating a map of their support system. Discuss the concept of a support system, and together read the introductory paragraph.
2. Either take instant photos of each teen, give out existing pictures, or allow teen(s) to draw a picture of themselves or just write their name in the circle in the center of the support map.
3. Instruct participant(s) to begin writing in the name and telephone number of people or organizations that are a part of their support system or they would like to be a part of their support system. Encourage teen(s) to use the checklist at the bottom of the page for ideas about people or organizations to put in their support map, but also encourage them to think of other support resources that are not listed. Aside from the teen's parents or primary caretakers, the support map should include adults who are not necessarily authority figures. It may include community-based organizations, which may be able to provide confidential or anonymous counseling and other services, and peers. Ask teen(s) if there is a situation they can imagine running into at some future date in which they might need help from a community organization. Use phone book to look up numbers of organizations that can meet that need - for example, if a teen were ever worried she might be pregnant, where could she get a free, confidential pregnancy test? Tell teen(s) to feel free to draw in more boxes if necessary, and encourage them to decorate the page any way they want.
4. Process by asking teen(s) how easy or difficult it is to ask for help and support with various issues. Ask for a volunteer to choose a situation in which it is difficult to ask for help, and role-play asking for help in that situation.

Facilitator's Note: When beginning the support map, teens may write the name of their dating partners first - this is fine and should not be discouraged. It is critical not to discount the importance of the partner, even in the most abusive relationships. Doing so will only alienate the teens you are trying to work with, and make it less likely that they will consider you part of their support systems. Instead, validate teens' feelings of being supported by their partners, and then move on to ask whom else they might include in their support systems. When the map is complete, the teens should be able to see that their partners are one of many support resources.

Use In Conjunction With:
SEALS+PLUS, *"No One is an "Is-land","* (page 63)
SEALS II, *"Supportive Relationships,"* (page 40)
SEALS III, *"Personal Network Profile,"* (page 80)
CROSSING THE BRIDGE, (pages 49, 50, 51)

Evaluating My Relationship

The purpose of this exercise is to help you start thinking about different aspects of your relationship. If you are not in a 'dating' relationship right now, focus on a past relationship or a present relationship with a friend or family member. Ask yourself the following questions about that person and your relationship with him or her.

I am evaluating my relationship with: _____

- Can you name five things about this person that you really like? 1. _____
  2. _____ 3. _____
  4. _____ 5. _____

- Can you name five things about this person that you really dislike? 1. _____
  2. _____ 3. _____
  4. _____ 5. _____

- Do you think this person's relationships with family and friends are healthy? Why or why not? _____
  _____

- Does this person encourage you to have other friends, or discourage other friendships? In what way? _____
  _____

- Can you name three things this person is interested in besides you? 1. _____
  2. _____ 3. _____

- Can you name three activities that you participate in without this person?
  1. _____
  2. _____ 3. _____

- Do you both have equal decision-making power in your relationship? _____

- How do the two of you usually handle conflicts? _____
  _____

- Since you have been in this relationship, do you generally feel better about yourself, worse about yourself, or about the same? _____

Facilitator's Information for
Evaluating My Relationship

Purpose: To explore positive and negative qualities of personal relationships.

Materials: One photocopy of worksheet per participant, plus one extra copy
Pens/pencils
Hat, box or bag

Activity (Group):
1. Cut up a photocopy of the worksheet into strips of paper with one question on each. Fold pieces of paper and put them into a hat, box or bag.
2. Seat participants in a circle.
3. Tell teens that the purpose of this activity is to begin to evaluate the different qualities of their relationships. Ask each participant to identify in his or her own mind a person who s/he has a relationship with - it can be an intimate partner, friend or family member. They do not have to tell the group who this person is. It may be a past relationship with an ex-boyfriend or girlfriend.
4. Ask for a group member to volunteer to be first. Instruct that group member to pick a piece of paper out of the hat and read it. After reading the question, go around the circle and ask each group member to answer the question to the best of his/her ability. The person who read the question goes last.
5. Repeat by having different group members pick and read aloud a question, going around the circle until each group member has answered each question.
6. Hand out worksheets and pens or pencils, and allow five or ten minutes for group members to fill in the blanks with the answers they gave during the group activity.

Activity (Individual):
1. Give teen the worksheet and a pen or pencil. Read or have teen read aloud the introductory paragraph.
2. Together with teen, read and discuss each question, instructing him or her to fill in the answers as you go along.
3. Process after completing the worksheet by discussing what aspects of the relationship the teen sees as positive or negative, which areas need change and how changes can be made.

Use In Conjunction With:
SEALS+PLUS, *"Roles,"* (page 49)
SEALS II, *"Supportive Relationships,"* (page 40)
SEALS III, *"Interview With,"* (page 33)
CROSSING THE BRIDGE, (pages 50, 51)

How Healthy Is My Relationship?

Following are two lists, one of healthy relationship characteristics and one of unhealthy traits. Many relationships have a combination of both. The point of this exercise is to figure out what things in your relationship are healthy or unhealthy, so you can gain appreciation for the best things and decide what you want to change. Read both lists, and check the heart next to every statement that is true about your relationship.

I am evaluating my relationship with: _____

IS IT HEALTHY?

Check the heart if you and this person...
- ♡ Have fun together more often than not
- ♡ Each enjoy spending time separately, with your own friends, as well as with each other's friends
- ♡ Always feel safe with each other
- ♡ Trust each other
- ♡ Are faithful to each other if you have made this commitment
- ♡ Support each other's individual goals in life, like getting a job or going to college
- ♡ Respect each other's opinions, even when they are different
- ♡ Solve conflicts without putting each other down, cursing at each other or making threats
- ♡ Both accept responsibility for your actions
- ♡ Both apologize when you're wrong
- ♡ Have equal decision-making power about what you do in your relationship
- ♡ Each control your own money
- ♡ Are proud to be with each other
- ♡ Encourage each other's interests - like sports & extracurricular activities
- ♡ Have some privacy - your letters, diary, personal phone calls are respected as your own
- ♡ Have close friends & family who like the other person and are happy about your relationship
- ♡ Never feel like you're being pressured for sex
- ♡ Communicate about sex, if your relationship is sexual
- ♡ Allow each other 'space' when you need it
- ♡ Always treat each other with respect

IS IT UNHEALTHY?

Check the heart if one of you...
- 💔 Gets extremely jealous or accuses the other of cheating
- 💔 Puts the other down by calling names, cursing or making the other feel bad about him or herself
- 💔 Yells at and treats the other like a child
- 💔 Doesn't take the other person, or things that are important to him/her, seriously
- 💔 Doesn't listen when the other talks
- 💔 Frequently criticizes the other's friends or family
- 💔 Pressures the other for sex, or makes sex hurt or feel humiliating
- 💔 Has ever threatened to hurt the other or commit suicide if they leave
- 💔 Cheats or threatens to cheat
- 💔 Tells the other how to dress
- 💔 Has ever grabbed, pushed, hit, or physically hurt the other
- 💔 Blames the other for your own behavior ("If you hadn't made me mad, I wouldn't have...")
- 💔 Embarrasses or humiliates the other
- 💔 Smashes, throws or destroys things
- 💔 Tries to keep the other from having a job or furthering his/her education
- 💔 Makes all the decisions about what the two of you do
- 💔 Tries to make the other feel crazy or plays mind games
- 💔 Goes back on promises
- 💔 Acts controlling or possessive - like you own your partner
- 💔 Uses alcohol or drugs as an excuse for hurtful behavior
- 💔 Ignores or withholds affection as a way of punishing the other
- 💔 Depends completely on the other to meet social or emotional needs

This list is a way of identifying some of the healthy and unhealthy characteristics of your relationship – it does not cover every possible situation. You may want to share this list with someone in your support system, and talk about where you want to make changes in your relationship and how you can begin to do this.

© 2001 Wellness Reproductions and Publishing, Inc. 1-800/669-9208

Facilitator's Information for
How Healthy Is My Relationship?

Purpose: To identify some of the healthy and unhealthy characteristics of participants' intimate relationships.

Materials: One photocopy of worksheet per participant
Pens/pencils

Activity (Group or Individual):
1. Introduce activity by stating this checklist is a way of understanding both the positive and negative sides of a relationship, and that most people have at least some checks on both sides.
2. Distribute worksheet(s) and pens/pencils.
3. Instruct teen(s) to identify the relationship they want to evaluate, and to write the name of that person in the box if they are comfortable doing so. (Identifying names should always be optional for reasons of confidentiality.) Specify that teen(s) may choose a dating partner, ex-partner, friend or family member.
4. Instruct participant(s) to take the time to read over the lists and check whichever items apply to their relationship most of the time. After they have completed the activity, review and discuss checked items with participants. In a group, ask for volunteers to share and discuss what they checked.
5. Ask teen(s) to identify which characteristics on the 'healthy' side are most important to them, and which characteristics on the 'unhealthy' side are most troubling and why.
6. Instruct participant(s) to circle any characteristic of their relationship they want to change.
7. Follow up with discussion/activity around making changes/goal planning. *[see below]*

Facilitator's Note: Many young people don't realize that certain controlling behaviors are abusive, but instead consider them 'romantic' — for example, they see jealousy as a sign of love rather than a sign of possessiveness. Having certain behaviors categorized as unhealthy will help them recognize them for what they are. It will also help them to realize that they are not the only ones in the world having these experiences. At the same time, it is important for victims of abuse to be able to identify some positive characteristics of their relationship, and to have others acknowledge that they are getting some needs met from their relationship. This activity will provide the counselor with a tool to engage young people in discussion about their intimate relationships.

Use In Conjunction With:
SEALS II, *"Savvy Socializing,"* (page 37)
SEALS II, *"Breaking Down Our Walls,"* (page 41)
SEALS II, *"Characteristics of Healthy Relationships,"* (page 42)
CROSSING THE BRIDGE, (pages 49, 50, 51)

QUIZ: What Would You Do...?

The purpose of this activity is to look at how you act in 'dating' relationships. After reading each situation, circle the letter next to the statement that best describes how you would act in that situation. Go with your first reaction, and try to be HONEST with yourself. The word 'partner' refers to your boyfriend or girlfriend.

1. **You're rushing down the hall because you're late for class. You see your partner outside the window talking to another guy/girl who you don't really know. They're both laughing. You:**
   A. Keep going to class - you're glad your partner seems to be having a good time.
   B. Keep going, but you can't help feeling a twinge of jealousy inside as you wonder if they were flirting. But you decide not to make an issue of it, because you trust your partner.
   C. Knock on the window and give your partner a look that says you don't want him/her talking to this person. You'll tell your partner that later.
   D. Go outside, grab your partner by the arm and drag him/her away while yelling accusations of flirting and maybe even cheating. You make it clear you don't ever want to see your partner around that person again, and if you do they will both get it!

2. **Your partner announces s/he is planning a night out with friends on Friday. You:**
   A. Tell your partner to have fun. You'll miss your regular Friday night together, but you haven't had a night out with your friends in a while either.
   B. Are a little hurt, and tell your partner you want to spend time together and thought s/he felt the same. After discussing it, you realize your partner does want to be with you but agree that both of your friendships are important too.
   C. Tell your partner "If you really loved me, you would want to spend all your time with me like I do with you." You know if you make him/her feel guilty enough you'll get your way.
   D. Get furious. You hate your partner's friends because they're always trying to break you two up, and you know s/he's probably planning to hook up with someone else. You tell your partner if s/he doesn't spend Friday with you, it's over.

3. **You and your partner usually go out to eat on Saturday nights. When it comes time to pay the bill:**
   A. You either split the bill or take turns paying, since you both have about the same amount of money.
   B. One of you pays most of the time, but this is mostly based on who has more money and not on 'gender roles.' The other person offers to pay when s/he can and this is comfortable for both people.
   C. The man in the relationship always pays, because this is how you both learned it's supposed to be.
   D. You always pay because you handle the money in this relationship. Besides, you know it means you can expect something in return later.

4. **You're alone with the person you've been going out with for a few weeks. You're fooling around and just when you're sure you're about to have sex, your partner stops and says s/he is not ready. You:**
   A. Stop immediately, even if you don't want to, because you respect your partner's decision.
   B. Are annoyed - now you're in the mood and you can't just turn it off. You may try to persuade your partner again, but you stop when it becomes clear s/he doesn't want to go any further.
   C. Try everything - make your partner feel guilty, say "I love you" even if you don't, call him/her a tease or a prude - anything that works to get your partner to agree to have sex with you.
   D. Don't take no for an answer. You've been going out long enough and done enough for your partner, so you deserve sex. If s/he won't say yes, you can do it anyway because you're stronger.

5. **Your partner cancelled plans with you because s/he has to work on a project in the library with a friend from English Class. Later one of your friends mentions he saw your partner sitting under a tree by the school with someone other than who your partner said s/he would be with. You:**
   A. Figure there must have been a change in plans and your partner will mention it later.
   B. Plan to ask your partner later how the library was. You know there's probably an explanation, but you want to make sure s/he's being honest with you.

(continued on next page)

QUIZ: What Would You Do...? (continued)

C. Question your friend about every detail, then angrily confront your partner and threaten the person s/he was talking to.
D. Blow your top - you know this means your partner is cheating on you. You take off to find them, so you can knock some sense into your partner and fight the person s/he's with.

6. Your partner just told you s/he's been accepted to a great college in another state. You:
A. Have been keeping your fingers crossed since you helped your partner with the college application, because you know this is a great opportunity even though you'll miss him/her.
B. Act happy, but can't help feeling disappointed. You had hoped your partner would go to a local school so you could be together.
C. Tell your partner s/he's making a mistake, will probably flunk out, and you might not be around when s/he gets back. You hope this will change his/her mind.
D. Tell your partner s/he's going over your dead body.

7. You want to go to the ball game, but your partner wants to go to a movie. You:
A. Compromise. You might go to the game tonight and go to the movie tomorrow, or decide to go your separate ways and meet up afterwards.
B. Try really hard to convince your partner to go to the game.
C. Get into an argument, and tell your partner you either go to the game or you don't go out at all.
D. Go to the game without discussion - you both know you make the decisions in the relationship.

8. Think about the worst argument you ever had with a dating partner. You:
A. Argued but did not 'hit below the belt' by calling each other nasty names or cursing each other out. In the end you either resolved the problem by talking, or agreed to disagree.
B. Got so angry that you cursed at your partner and said some hurtful things - but never intimidated or made your partner feel unsafe.
C. Got so angry that you punched a wall or broke something.
D. Got so angry that you grabbed, pushed or hit your partner.

Evaluate Your Answers

If you had all A's (and you were honest), you seem to have a very healthy attitude about intimate relationships. You believe both partners are equal, and share equal decision-making power and equal responsibility. You also respect each other's rights, beliefs and decisions, and support each other's goals. You should share your values with your peers as often as possible, be a role model for friends by continuing to treat others with respect, and speak up when people are disrespectful.

If you had A's and B's, you believe in equality in relationships and your attitude is relatively healthy - but sometimes, maybe without even meaning to, you might try to manipulate situations in your favor instead of respecting your partner's ability to make the best decision for him/herself. Figure out what role jealousy plays in your relationship, and just try to be conscious of your feelings and actions. Be a role model and speak up with your peers about healthy relationships.

If you had any C's, this is where you have crossed the line from occasional feelings of jealousy or insecurity to behaving in ways that are controlling and verbally or emotionally abusive. It is important that you talk to a counselor to understand this controlling behavior better, before it turns into a major pattern.

If you had more than a couple of C's, you have probably begun a pattern of controlling your partner through manipulation, intimidation, isolation and by making him/her feel badly about him/herself. This kind of behavior is emotionally abusive, and could escalate to physical abuse. You should take a serious look at your behavior and talk with a counselor about it.

If you had any D's, you are either in a physically abusive relationship or in a very emotionally abusive relationship. Your attitudes towards relationships are unhealthy for you and your partner. The more D's you have, the more abusive you are. It is very important that you talk to a counselor so they can help you re-evaluate your attitudes and behaviors now, while you're young, before you get 'set in your ways.'

Facilitator's Information for
QUIZ: What Would You Do...?

Purpose: To assess one's own behavior for healthy and abusive tendencies.
To identify a range of responses to common situations in teen dating relationships.

Materials: One photocopy of worksheet per participant
Pens/pencils

Activity (Group or Individual):
1. Introduce the activity by telling the teen(s) that you would like them to take this 'quiz' to see how they tend to respond to certain situations in relationships.
2. Review vocabulary as necessary, including 'partner,' 'gender roles,' and 'emotional abuse.'
3. Ask the teen(s) to take the quiz on their own, or read it aloud together and have them choose the answer that corresponds to how they think they would most likely respond.
4. Have teen(s) count up the number of A's, B's, C's, and D's they circled, and see how many they have of each letter. Read and discuss the description that applies to their answers. Go back and discuss individual responses, and discuss with the teen(s) how their responses are controlling or healthy.

(Group): (This activity may be done by itself or as a follow-up to the above activity.)
1. Split the group into smaller groups of two to four people. Assign each group a number from 1-8.
2. Give each group a copy of the 'quiz' with the question number circled that corresponds to the group number.
3. Tell each group that it has about 10 minutes to develop a role-play based on the scenario circled on their quiz. Group members can choose to play out any one of the responses described in the quiz, or make up a different response on their own. Specify that they do not have to role-play the situation how they would personally handle it, and they are not necessarily required to show a healthy or abusive relationship. The only rule is that if they are going to act out violence, there can be no actual physical contact.
4. After each group has developed its role-play, have the groups perform their role-plays one at a time. After a group has acted out its role-play, ask the audience members how healthy or unhealthy they felt the response was, and why. If it was unhealthy, ask for volunteers from the audience to replace the actors and respond to the situation in a healthier way.
5. After each group has performed its role-play and unhealthy behaviors have been 'corrected' by the audience, process by discussing how easy or difficult it is in real life to change your own patterns of behavior. Point out that this activity shows that there are always a number of different choices about how to react to difficult situations, and while violence may be one option, there are also other, healthier options.

Use In Conjunction With:
SEALS+PLUS, *"Self-Disclosure,"* (page 14)
SEALS II, *"Savvy Socializing,"* (page 37)
SEALS III, *"Understanding the Ripple Effect,"* (page 63)

Different Types of Relationships

1. Listed in the box below are different types of relationships. Pick six different relationships and write them in the shapes. Then write the names of two people who have that type of relationship.

2. Next, think about the different things these two people get out of the relationship. These could be emotional needs, social satisfactions or basic necessities like food and shelter. Write a few of the things the relationship provides.

EXAMPLES OF DIFFERENT TYPES OF RELATIONSHIPS			
Friendship	*Teammate*	*Boyfriend/Girlfriend*	*Boss-Worker*
Acquaintance	*Mentor*	*Neighbor*	*Co-worker*
Parent-Child	*Sibling*	*Teacher-Student*	*Classmate*

Type of Relationship
_____
Between
_____ & _____
Provides
_____
_____

Type of Relationship
_____
Between
_____ & _____
Provides
_____
_____

Type of Relationship
_____
Between
_____ & _____
Provides
_____
_____

Type of Relationship
_____
Between
_____ & _____
Provides
_____
_____
_____
_____

Type of Relationship
_____
Between
_____ & _____
Provides
_____
_____
_____
_____

Type of Relationship
_____
Between
_____ & _____
Provides
_____
_____

Facilitator's Information for
Different Types of Relationships

Purpose: To identify some of the different needs that are met by different types of relationships.
To emphasize the importance of a diverse support network.

Materials: One photocopy of worksheet per participant
Pens, pencils or fine-tipped markers
Additional for GROUP: Flipchart and markers/blackboard and chalk

Activity (Group):
1. Introduce activity by asking participants to define the word 'relationship.' After hearing participants' ideas, offer this simple definition: A connection between two or more people. Discuss the idea that a relationship does not have to mean an intimate relationship, but that there are many different kinds of relationships that serve many different purposes.
2. Write the following sentence on the board or flip-chart and ask each group member to complete the sentence: "In my relationship with _____, I get the following needs met: _____."
3. Prompt teens to brainstorm as many different types of relationships as they can think of. This may be done as one group or by breaking participants up into smaller groups, then reconvening the group to combine lists. Write the list on flip chart or board.
4. Distribute worksheets and pens/pencils/markers.
5. Read or have a teen read aloud the directions.
6. Instruct teens to fill in the shapes with types of relationships and the names of people in those relationships. Encourage teens to use relationships of their own, although they may also use relationships of two other people they know, celebrities or characters from a TV show, movie or book.
7. Ask teens to think about what the people they named get out of the relationship. For example, someone to talk to, someone to play ball with, a job, help with homework, etc.
8. Encourage participants to decorate the page with markers if desired. Facilitator may instruct teens to use certain colors to indicate which relationships are most important, which relationships meet certain types of needs, which relationships have stronger or weaker boundaries, etc.
9. Process this activity with the following questions:
   * What was the purpose of this activity?
   * How does this activity relate to the idea of a support system?
   * What relationships help you meet your social needs? Your survival needs? Your educational needs? Your emotional needs?
   * Are there types of relationships that participants don't have but would like to have? If so, how would you go about developing these types of relationships?

Activity (Individual):
1. Introduce activity with a discussion of the meaning of the word 'relationship,' as in #1 above.
2. Assist teen in developing a list of different types of relationships, either verbally or on paper.
3. Give participant a copy of the worksheet, and work with him or her to fill in each of the shapes with examples of each type of relationship and the kinds of needs they meet, as in numbers 6-8 above.
4. Process as in #9 above.

Use In Conjunction With:
SEALS+PLUS, *"Influential People...,"* (page 51)
SEALS II, *"Energizing vs. Draining,"* (page 36)
SEALS III, *"Creative Love, Creating Love,"* (page 49)
CROSSING THE BRIDGE, (pages 50)

3 Kinds of Love

According to one theory*, there are three different kinds of love. After reading descriptions of each kind of love, think about whether you have experienced that kind of love. Write examples of your experiences with each kind of love in the spaces provided.

Romantic Love (A.K.A. "The Honeymoon Stage")

Most relationships start out with romantic love. During this stage, everything about the relationship and the other person seems perfect. Both partners usually try to show only their better sides, and unattractive traits are either not recognized, or they are redefined so that they seem like positive characteristics. For example, instead of viewing your partner as 'selfish,' you might see them as 'independent,' instead of 'stubborn' you see them as 'determined.' Often the early warning signs of controlling behavior, like extreme jealousy and possessiveness, are misunderstood as a sign of love and devotion. Both partners want to be together all of the time, and this is also seen as proof of true love.

In most cases, reality sets in eventually and both partners begin to see each other's faults. At this point, the relationship can grow into a 'nurturing' or an 'addictive' relationship.

Write about your experiences with Romantic Love:

_____
_____
_____
_____
_____
_____
_____
_____
_____
_____
_____
_____
_____
_____
_____
_____
_____
_____
_____
_____

(continued on next page)

3 Kinds of Love

(continued)

Nurturing Love (A.K.A. "Healthy Relationship")

Nurturing Love is when Romantic Love matures into a deeper, more complicated relationship. Both people appreciate each other's positive qualities, but also recognize and accept each other's limitations. Both partners want the other to grow and develop to her or his fullest potential. This means that they encourage each other to have other close friendships and to get satisfaction out of independent activities. In Nurturing Love, one partner is even able to accept when the other wants to spend more time apart. If one person ends the relationship, the other will experience sadness and grief, but will not be devastated to the point of being self-destructive or unable to function.

Write about your experiences with Nurturing Love:

(continued on next page)

3 Kinds of Love

(continued)

Addictive Love (A.K.A. "An Abusive Relationship")

When the desire to be together every minute turns into a feeling of extreme need for the partner to be constantly available, Romantic Love has turned into Addictive Love. One or both partners say things like, "I'll die if he doesn't call me," "I can't live without her," "She's everything to me." Addictive love is a learned behavior, and males and females often show their 'addiction' differently because of their learned gender roles. Gender roles have defined females as emotional and needy, so often dependency on a partner is seen as natural and practical. However, because dependence does not fit with a 'manly' image, males are less likely to admit to being 'hooked.' Instead, a male may claim he does not need his partner, yet he feels a desperate need to keep her close so he tries to control her. He often does this by putting her down, insisting she has no right to 'neglect' him, calling her selfish, and threatening to break up with her.

In a male-female couple, the way the male shows his 'addiction' through criticism may lead the female to believe the problems in the relationship are her fault. She may also believe that he doesn't need her, so she becomes insecure about herself and the relationship. She narrows the focus of her life to concentrate on pleasing him, and has an exaggerated idea of how necessary he is to her life. She feels like she is addicted to him, and does not realize her power to make healthy choices.

Write about your experiences with Addictive Love:

___

Signs of Addictive Love are listed below. Check any that you see in yourself or your partner.

❑ A person believes he or she "can't live without" the other person.

❑ Less and less of the couple's time together is happy, interesting or satisfying. More and more time is spent arguing, apologizing, making promises, expressing anger, feeling guilty and being afraid of upsetting the other.

❑ Lowered feelings of self-worth (self-esteem) and self-control.

❑ A person is unable to enjoy time away from his or her partner, and when apart is always "counting the minutes" until they are together again.

❑ A person often makes and breaks promises to him or herself to limit dependency on the partner ("I won't call him," "I won't ask her where she's been," "I won't wait for the phone to ring.")

❑ A feeling of never being able to get enough of the other person.

❑ Increasing efforts to control the other person.

Facilitator's Information for
3 Kinds of Love

Purpose: To understand the difference between romantic love, nurturing love and addictive love.

Materials: One photocopy of each of the three worksheets per participant
Pens/pencils
Optional: Flipchart and markers/blackboard and chalk

Activity (Group or Individual):

1. Distribute one of each worksheet and a pen or pencil to each teen.
2. Read or have participant(s) read aloud the explanation for each of the three kinds of love, discussing terms and concepts as necessary. Point out that each kind of love has an "A.K.A." next to it, referring to concepts members may have discussed in the past or may discuss in future sessions (activities in "Understanding Abuse" section of this workbook.). Ask participants to discuss these concepts.
3. After reading each section, ask teen(s) if they can think of examples from their own lives, or from relationships in movies or television shows. Instruct participant(s) to write these examples in the space provided. If working with a group, allow group members to share their examples if they are comfortable doing so.
4. When discussing Addictive Love, clarify that the term 'Addictive' is used because the people involved have feelings of extreme dependency. However, it is not a true addiction in the sense of chemical dependency. Abusive behavior can not be justified by calling it an 'addiction'. Abusers are still making a <u>choice</u> to use abusive tactics to gain power and control over their partners.
5. Read or have a participant read aloud the "Signs of Addictive Love." Instruct participant(s) to check any signs that they see in their current relationships, or a past relationship if they are not currently in one.
6. Process with a discussion of what one can do to 'steer' a new relationship in the direction of nurturing love rather than addictive love. Facilitator may write a list of participant(s)' ideas on flipchart or blackboard.

Use In Conjunction With:
SEALS+PLUS, *"Balance Your Life,"* (page 69)
SEALS II, *"Keeping Our Commitments,"* (page 43)
SEALS III, *"Process of Making Changes,"* (page 40)

* Adapted from "Addictive Love and Abuse: A Course for Teenage Women" by Ginny NiCarthy, in <u>Dating Violence: Young Women in Danger</u>, edited by Barrie Levy, The Seal Press, 1991.

How My Relationship Affects My Life

Ask yourself the following questions about how your relationship is affecting important areas of your life. Then think about any areas where you want to make changes, and talk with someone in your support system about how you can do this.

I am evaluating my relationship with: _____

SCHOOL:
- Does this person encourage me to do well in school? _____
- Have my grades improved, fallen or stayed the same since I've been in this relationship? _____
- Does this person pressure me to skip school? _____
- Have I ever missed or been late to school because of a fight with this person? _____
- Have I ever quit a school group or club so I could spend that time with this person? _____
- If I want to go to college, does this person support this goal? _____

WORK:
- Does this person support me in my job/career? _____
- Have I ever missed or been late to work because of a fight with this person? _____
- Does this person pressure me to miss work? _____
- Do I talk to this person on the phone so much while at work that it gets in the way of my job? _____
- Has this person ever shown up at my job to 'check up' on me because of jealousy? _____
  If so, has this caused me embarrassment or questions from co-workers or boss? _____

MY PHYSICAL HEALTH:
- Have I ever had cuts, bruises, or other injuries as a result of a fight with this person? _____
- Have I gained or lost a significant amount of weight since I've been in this relationship? _____
- Have I ever contracted a sexually transmitted disease from this person? _____
- Have I had any unplanned pregnancies from this relationship? _____
- Have I ever been so upset about a fight with this person that I became physically ill? _____
- Does this person ever threaten me physically or do dangerous things, like driving recklessly with me in the car? _____

(continued on next page)

How My Relationship Affects My Life (continued)

MY EMOTIONAL HEALTH (LEVEL OF STRESS, FEELINGS OF SELF WORTH):

- Do I feel better about myself or worse about myself since I have been in this relationship? _____
- Do I ever think that "I am nothing" without this person - that I couldn't go on without him or her? _____
- Do I feel more or less stressed, depressed or anxious? _____
- Do I cry more or less frequently since I've been in this relationship? _____
- Do I have more trouble sleeping at night or sleep more than usual since I've been in this relationship? _____

USE OF DRUGS/ALCOHOL:

- Have I started/increased or stopped/decreased smoking, drinking or using drugs since I've been in this relationship? _____
- Does this person pressure me to use drugs or alcohol? _____
- Do I ever use drugs/alcohol to help myself calm down or feel better after a fight? _____
- Do I ever use drugs/alcohol because I feel it will "loosen me up" and make me less inhibited around this person or around his/her friends? _____

MY FAMILY & FRIENDSHIPS:

- How do my friends & family feel about this person? How does this person feel about them? _____
- Have I grown apart from my friends & family since I've been in this relationship, or gotten closer? _____
- Does this person ever act jealous of my friends/family and try to keep me away from them? _____
- Has this person ever threatened or gotten into a physical fight with a friend or family member? _____
- Has this person pressured me to quit a club, group or team? _____
- Do I find myself lying to my friends & family to cover up for this person? _____
- Do we each spend time separately with our own friends? _____

MY ABILITY TO FUNCTION INDEPENDENTLY:

- Do I have control of my own money? _____
- Have my living arrangements become dependent on this person? _____
- Do I ever feel that I could not 'make it' without this person? _____
- In what other ways, positive or negative, do I think this relationship has affected my life? _____

Facilitator's Information for
How My Relationship Affects My Life

Purpose: To identify and explore the negative and positive affects of participants relationships on functioning in other important areas of their lives.

Materials: One photocopy of worksheet per participant
Pens/pencils
Optional: Flipchart and markers/blackboard and chalk

Activity (Group or Individual):

1. Introduce the activity by asking participant(s): "Have you ever gotten so caught up in your love life that it seems like nothing else exists?" Explain that it's normal, in the beginning of a romantic relationship, to go through a period where you think about almost nothing else. But in a healthy relationship, you should begin to come back to reality after a few weeks or so and integrate the relationship into other areas of your life, rather than allowing the relationship to take over everything else. It's important that we don't neglect the other important areas of our life like family, friends, school and health. State that the purpose of this activity is to take a look at what kind of impact our relationships are having on these other things.
2. Ask participant(s) to brainstorm a list of other areas in their lives besides their love life. Write list on flipchart or blackboard, if desired.
3. Distribute handout(s) and pens/pencils. Instruct participant(s) to read each question, or read questions as a group, and answer them as honestly as possible.
4. After completing the handout, ask participant(s) to identify areas where they think their relationship is having a positive or negative affect on their lives. From there, generate discussion about specific changes they would like to make in areas where there is a negative impact.
5. If participant(s) have identified specific areas for change, follow up with discussion/activities on making changes/goal setting.

Use In Conjunction With:
SEALS II, *"Relationships & You,"* (page 35)
SEALS II, *"Energizing & Draining,"* (page 36)
SEALS III, *"Understanding the Ripple Effect,"* (page 63)

Balancing You, Me and Us

It's a romantic idea that when two people are in love they become one - but in reality, that way of thinking can sometimes be unhealthy. Another way to look at relationships is that two people, ME and YOU, overlap to create a third part of a relationship - US. If one of those three parts dominates, the other parts get neglected.

For example, if the relationship's all about ME, then I am focused on getting my needs met and expect you to make my needs your priority too - but your needs suffer.

If the relationship's all about YOU, then I might spend all my energy trying to please you, but I do not take care of my own needs.

If the relationship is all about US, then we are both focused so intensely on the relationship that we each lose our individual identities.

In a healthy relationship, the ME, YOU and US are in balance most of the time. There might be days when I am having a problem so we focus on me, or you are celebrating a special accomplishment so we focus on you. But as a whole, we are able to achieve a balance between ME, YOU and US.

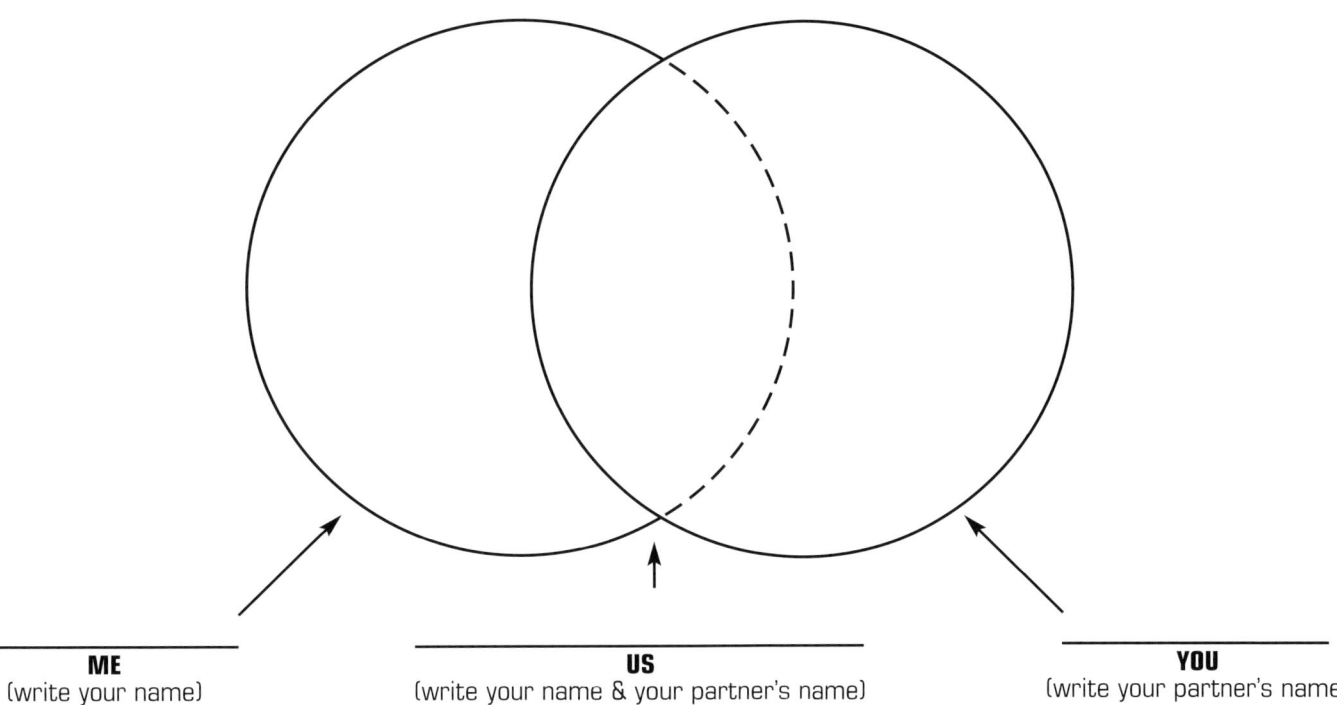

ME
(write your name)

US
(write your name & your partner's name)

YOU
(write your partner's name)

The overlapping circles above represent the three parts of a relationship - ME, YOU and US. Write your name and the name of your partner under the left and right circles. In the part of the circle that represents only you, write the things that are a part of you as an individual - for example, your close friends, family members, activities you enjoy by yourself, your education or career goals, talents and hobbies that are uniquely yours. Then do the same for your partner. In the center, where the two circles overlap to represent the US in your relationship, write things that you and your partner share together: special feelings, activities you enjoy together, friends that you have in common, special memories or future plans.

Now ask yourself: Are the Me, You and Us in your relationship in balance? _____
If not, which part(s) need more attention? _____

Facilitator's Information for
Balancing You, Me and Us

Purpose: To understand the importance of maintaining balance between one's self and one's partner in a relationship.
To identify and differentiate between aspects of each partner as an individual and aspects of the shared relationship.

Materials: One photocopy of worksheet per participant
Thin-tipped, colored markers
Additional for GROUP: Flipchart and markers/blackboard and chalk

Activity (Group):
1. Begin activity by stating that there are three parts of a relationship: the first is ME, the second is YOU . . . ask participants what they think the third part is. When a participant has answered US or facilitator has given the answer, write ME on the left side of flip chart or board, YOU on the right side, and US in the middle.
2. Ask participants "Which one of these do you think should dominate in a healthy relationship?" Most participants will probably answer US. Ask reasons why, and then ask participants if they think there are negative effects when both people in the relationship focus only on the US in the relationship and not on the ME or YOU.
3. After discussion, state that in a healthy relationship, none of those three parts dominates, but each of the three parts are in balance. Draw circles around ME and YOU so that they overlap over the US, as in the illustration on the worksheet.
4. Distribute worksheets and markers, and read or have participants read the top part of the page, discussing as necessary.
5. Read the directions below the large circles and instruct participants to fill in their names and names of their partners (or ex-partners, friends or family members.) Instruct teens to fill in the circles as directed, encouraging them to use words or pictures and to decorate the circles as they wish.
6. Instruct teens to complete the two questions at the bottom of the page.
7. Ask for volunteers to share what they wrote, or, in an intimate group, ask for anyone who is comfortable having their answers read aloud to hand in worksheets. Without identifying whose worksheet it is, read the words in the ME circle and see if other participants can guess who it is.
8. Process with the following questions:
   • What are some of the consequences of having poorly balanced relationships?
   • In an abusive relationship, which part of the relationship dominates?
   • If anyone has discovered that their relationship is out of balance, what can you do to change the balance, (a) if the ME dominates, (b) if the YOU dominates, or (c) if the US dominates.
9. Follow up with discussion/activity on making changes or goal planning - see "Use In Conjunction With" below.

Activity (Individual):
1. Give teen worksheet and markers, and together read the top part of the page, discussing as necessary.
2. Read the directions below the large circles and instruct teen to fill in his or her name and the name of his or her partner (or ex-partner, friend, family member.)
3. Prompt teen to write in the circles as described to identify parts of his/her individual self, partner's individual self, as well as aspects of their shared selves. Encourage teen to use colorful markers to write words or draw pictures, and to decorate the circles any way they wish.
4. Once teen has filled in the circles as much as possible, ask him or her whether s/he thinks the ME, YOU and US in his or her relationship are in balance, and why or why not.
5. Instruct teen to answer the two questions at the bottom of the page.
6. Process with questions as in #8 above.
7. Follow up with discussion/activity on making changes or goal planning - see activities listed below.

Use In Conjunction With:
SEALS+PLUS, *"What Do I Value,"* (page 72)
SEALS+PLUS, *"One Step at a Time,"* (page 32)
SEALS II, *"Reward Yourself,"* (page 29) SEALS II, *"Treat Yourself,"* (page 30)
SEALS III, *"Goal/Obstacle/Plan,"* (page 18)
CROSSING THE BRIDGE, (pages 49, 50)

Myths & Facts
on Domestic Violence & Teen Relationship Abuse

On the line next to each statement, check "M" if you think the statement is a myth, or "F" if you think it is fact. After taking this survey, when you are given the answers, write the FACTS about the issue on the line below each statement.

1. Domestic violence usually only happens in married adult couples. M. _____ F. _____
   _____

2. Boyfriends and girlfriends sometimes push each other around when they get angry, but it rarely results in anyone getting seriously hurt. M. _____ F. _____
   _____

3. While females can be abusive and abuse happens in same-sex couples too, it is much more common for males to abuse their female partners. M. _____ F. _____
   _____

4. If a mother is abused by her children's father, the children are also likely to be abused. M. _____ F. _____
   _____

5. Most people will end a relationship if their boyfriend or girlfriend hits them. M. _____ F. _____
   _____

6. People abuse their partners because they can't control their anger. M. _____ F. _____
   _____

7. Most men who abuse their partners grew up in violent homes. M. _____ F. _____
   _____

8. If a person is really being abused, it's easy to just leave. M. _____ F. _____
   _____

9. Most rapes are committed by strangers who attack women at night on the streets. M. _____ F. _____
   _____

10. A pregnant woman is at an even greater risk of physical abuse. M. _____ F. _____
    _____

11. Relationship abuse happens most often among blacks and Hispanics. M. _____ F. _____
    _____

12. People who are abused often blame themselves for their abuse. M. _____ F. _____
    _____

(continued on next page)

Myths & Facts on Domestic Violence & Teen Relationship Abuse (continued)

MYTH OR FACT?   **FACT SHEET**

1. M.
   FACT: As many as one-third of all high school and college-age young people experience violence in an intimate or dating relationship.[1] Physical abuse is as common among high school and college-age couples as married couples.[2]

2. M.
   FACT: Domestic violence is the number one cause of injury to women between the ages of 15-44 in the U.S. - more than car accidents, muggings and rapes combined.[3] Of the women murdered each year in the U.S., 30% are killed by their current or former husband or boyfriend.[4]

3. F.
   FACT: About 95% of known victims of relationship violence are females abused by their male partners.[5]

4. F.
   FACT: 50% of men who frequently abuse their wives also frequently abuse their children.[6] A child who lives in a family where there is violence between parents is 15 times more likely to be abused.[7]

5. M.
   FACT: Nearly 80% of girls who have been physically abused in their intimate relationships continue to date their abuser after the onset of violence.[8]

6. M.
   FACT: People who abuse are usually not out of control. They do it to gain power and control over the other person. They often use a series of tactics besides violence, including threats, intimidation, psychological abuse and isolation to control their partners.[9]

7. F.
   FACT: Men who have witnessed violence between parents are three times more likely to abuse their own wives and children than children of non-violent parents. The sons of the most violent parents are 1000 times more likely to become batterers.[10]

8. M.
   FACT: There are many very complicated reasons why it's difficult for a person to leave an abusive partner. (see worksheet <u>Why People Stay in Abusive Relationships</u>.) One very common reason is fear - women who leave their abusers are at a 75% greater chance of being killed by the abuser than those who stay.[11]

9. M.
   FACT: About 80% of rapes and sexual assaults are committed by a partner, friend or acquaintance of the victim.[12]

10. F.
    FACT: Pregnant women are especially at risk for abuse. It is estimated that more than one-third of pregnant women are abused.[13] It is common for physical abuse to begin or escalate during pregnancy.

11. M.
    FACT: Women of all races are equally likely to be abused by a partner.[14]

12. F.
    FACT: Most people who are abused blame themselves for causing the violence.[15] However, the fact is that NO ONE is ever to blame for another person's violence - violence is always a choice, and the responsibility is 100% with the person who is violent.

Facilitator's Information for
Myths & Facts on Domestic Violence & Teen Relationship Abuse

Purpose: To dispel some common myths and understand facts about relationship abuse.

Materials: One photocopy of worksheet per participant
Pens/pencils
Additional for GROUP: Four pieces of 8½ x 11 paper with "MYTH" printed largely on two pieces, and "FACT" printed largely on the other two pieces.
Prizes or incentives for winning team

Activity (Group):
1. Introduce activity as a 'Game Show' to test participants' knowledge of myths and facts about teen relationship abuse and domestic violence. Facilitator can play the role of the game show host, or have a group member volunteer to play the host.
2. Split the group into two teams.
3. Tell teens that the host will make a statement about teen relationship abuse or domestic violence, and the teams will be given thirty seconds to discuss with their teammates and decide whether the statement is a myth or a fact. (Facilitator may need to review the meaning of the word 'myth.')
4. When the host calls 'time' after 30 seconds, a member of each team must hold up one of the signs - MYTH or FACT. A team that does not hold up its sign right away forfeits its chance to win points. If both teams get the right answer, they each get one point. If only one team gets the right answer, that team earns two points.
5. Optionally, facilitator may give teams the chance to win 'bonus points' if they can say why the statement is a myth or a fact. They do not have to guess the exact statistics, but demonstrate an understanding of the general concept behind the fact, at the facilitator's discretion.
6. After the game show is over award prizes and distribute worksheets and pens/pencils. Read over each statement and the corresponding facts from the "Fact Sheet," and instruct participants to fill in the facts, in their own words, under each statement.

Activity (Individual):
1. Give teen worksheet and pen/pencil.
2. Review the meaning of the word 'myth,' if necessary.
3. Either instruct teen to complete the survey on his/her own, or read each statement together and ask teen whether s/he thinks the statement is a myth or fact.
4. After completing the worksheet, take out the "Fact Sheet" and review the answers and corresponding facts for each statement. Instruct teen to write in the facts in the space provided as you go along.

Use In Conjunction With:
SEALS+PLUS, *"Opening Doors to Achievement,"* (page 43)
SEALS II, *"Envisioning Female Role Models,"* (page 49)
SEALS II, *"Envisioning Male Role Models,"* (page 50)

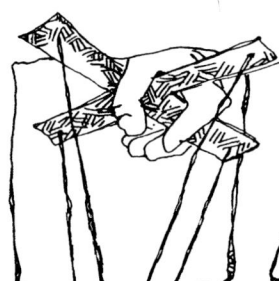

Understanding Power & Control Tactics

Consider the following definition of abuse: *"Abuse is any attempt to gain power or control over another person using physical, emotional or sexual tactics."* The 'Wheel' you see on this page shows that Power and Control are at the center of an abusive relationship. In other words, abuse is when there is a pattern of one person trying to gain power and control over the other. One of the most obvious or blatant ways to control another person is by using violence – such as hitting a person, holding them down or sexually assaulting someone. However there are other ways of controlling a person that do not include physical violence and are not so easy to spot. Instead of using physical or sexual violence, many abusers may use verbal, emotional, psychological or financial tactics to control the other person. Some examples of these forms of abuse are shown in between the 'spokes' of the wheel. They are more subtle (not so obvious) so often people do not recognize them as abuse. But they are abuse, and they often lead to physical violence.

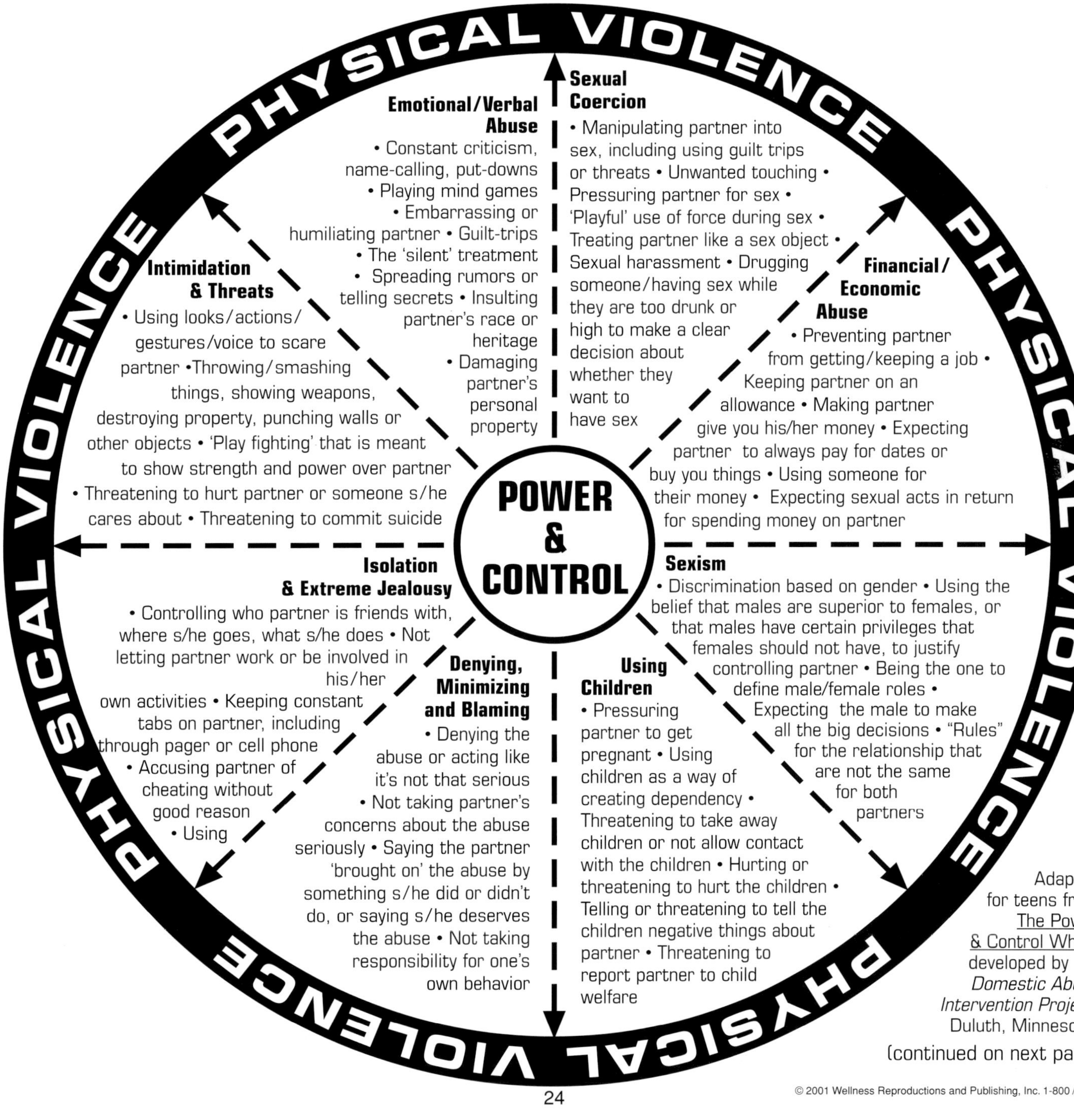

PHYSICAL VIOLENCE

POWER & CONTROL

Emotional/Verbal Abuse
- Constant criticism, name-calling, put-downs
- Playing mind games
- Embarrassing or humiliating partner
- Guilt-trips
- The 'silent' treatment
- Spreading rumors or telling secrets
- Insulting partner's race or heritage
- Damaging partner's personal property

Sexual Coercion
- Manipulating partner into sex, including using guilt trips or threats
- Unwanted touching
- Pressuring partner for sex
- 'Playful' use of force during sex
- Treating partner like a sex object
- Sexual harassment
- Drugging someone/having sex while they are too drunk or high to make a clear decision about whether they want to have sex

Financial/Economic Abuse
- Preventing partner from getting/keeping a job
- Keeping partner on an allowance
- Making partner give you his/her money
- Expecting partner to always pay for dates or buy you things
- Using someone for their money
- Expecting sexual acts in return for spending money on partner

Sexism
- Discrimination based on gender
- Using the belief that males are superior to females, or that males have certain privileges that females should not have, to justify controlling partner
- Being the one to define male/female roles
- Expecting the male to make all the big decisions
- "Rules" for the relationship that are not the same for both partners

Using Children
- Pressuring partner to get pregnant
- Using children as a way of creating dependency
- Threatening to take away children or not allow contact with the children
- Hurting or threatening to hurt the children
- Telling or threatening to tell the children negative things about partner
- Threatening to report partner to child welfare

Denying, Minimizing and Blaming
- Denying the abuse or acting like it's not that serious
- Not taking partner's concerns about the abuse seriously
- Saying the partner 'brought on' the abuse by something s/he did or didn't do, or saying s/he deserves the abuse
- Not taking responsibility for one's own behavior

Isolation & Extreme Jealousy
- Controlling who partner is friends with, where s/he goes, what s/he does
- Not letting partner work or be involved in his/her own activities
- Keeping constant tabs on partner, including through pager or cell phone
- Accusing partner of cheating without good reason
- Using

Intimidation & Threats
- Using looks/actions/gestures/voice to scare partner
- Throwing/smashing things, showing weapons, destroying property, punching walls or other objects
- 'Play fighting' that is meant to show strength and power over partner
- Threatening to hurt partner or someone s/he cares about
- Threatening to commit suicide

Adapted for teens from *The Power & Control Wheel* developed by the *Domestic Abuse Intervention Project*, Duluth, Minnesota.

(continued on next page)

Understanding Power & Control Tactics (continued)

Each sentence below is an example of one of the tactics described in the "Power and Control" wheel on the previous page. Draw a line to match the example on the left to the "Power and Control" tactic on the right.

1. Jason has never hit Pat, but when he's angry he often scares Pat by punching walls or throwing things.

2. David makes Keira quit her job because he doesn't trust the guys she works with. Instead, he says he'll give her a weekly allowance – as long as she's "good."

3. Denise tells William that if he leaves her, she'll make sure that she gets full custody of their son and she will never let William see him.

4. After hitting her, Robin tells Kim to stop crying and making such a big deal out of nothing, adding "I just get so out of control when I see you flirting with other people like that. If you didn't act like that I wouldn't have to hurt you."

5. Rosario bad-mouths Kristin's friends all the time. Finally, he tells her he doesn't want her hanging out with them anymore because they're all a bunch of 'hoes.

6. Eva wants to have sex and Lynell isn't ready. Eva says if he doesn't want her, she'll have to tell everyone he's gay, and get her sexual needs met by a 'real man'.

7. Dillan and Dee are eating dinner with friends when Dillan says jokingly to Dee, "Are you sure you're gonna have dessert? I don't know, baby, that stuff is going right to your butt."

8. While Kian listens to his girlfriend's ideas, he expects that he should always make the final decisions because he is the man.

A. Isolation & Extreme Jealousy

B. Denying, Minimizing and Blaming

C. Using Children

D. Sexism

E. Financial/Economic Abuse

F. Sexual Coercion

G. Intimidation & Threats

H. Emotional/Verbal Abuse

Facilitator's Information for
Understanding Power & Control Tactics

Purpose: To identify and understand some of the many different tactics abusers use to gain power and control over their partners.

Materials: One photocopy of each worksheet per participant
Pens/pencils
Additional for GROUP: Flipchart and markers/blackboard and chalk.
One additional copy of second worksheet, cut up into eight pieces of paper with one situation on each paper.
Tape

Activity (Group:)
1. Ahead of time, draw a large outline of the wheel on blackboard or flip-chart with the headings for each section written in.
2. Distribute first worksheet, the 'wheel' of power & control. Review the wheel visually, explaining that the center is power and control, because abusive relationships are based on one person wanting power and control over the other. In between the "spokes" of the wheel are the behaviors abusers use to gain power and control. On the outside of the wheel is the physical violence, because that is the most visible and extreme way of gaining power and control. Often, the tactics inside the wheel lead to physical violence.
3. Review each section of the wheel, reading the heading and the examples listed on the worksheet. Ask group members if they can think of any examples in their own lives, in the lives of people they know, or in TV shows or movies.
4. Pass out pieces of paper with scenarios from second worksheet. If you have more than 8 group members, you can make up additional examples, or just ask for 8 group members to volunteer.
5. Ask each group member with a paper to read his or her scenario aloud, decide where on the wheel that example falls and tape the piece of paper on the large wheel. Ask the rest of the group if they agree, and if not, where they think it should go.
6. Repeat this with each scenario until there is an example taped to each section of the wheel. Provide "answer key" and review the answers.
7. Distribute photocopies of second worksheet and instruct teens to draw a line from each scenario to the tactic it represents.
8. After teens have finished matching the examples to the behavior, provide the 'answer key' and review each answer, explaining any mistakes.

Activity (Individual:)
1. Give teen the copy of first worksheet and read or have teen read aloud the explanation above the power and control wheel.
2. Review the wheel visually first, explaining that the center is power and control, because abusive relationships are based on one person wanting power and control over the other. In between the 'spokes' of the wheel are the behaviors abusers use to gain power and control. On the outside of the wheel is the physical violence, because that is the most visible and extreme way of gaining power and control. Often, the tactics inside the wheel lead to physical violence.
3. Review each section of the wheel, first reading the examples listed and then asking the teen if s/he can think of any examples in his or her life, in the lives of people s/he knows, or in TV shows or movies.
4. After reviewing the wheel, give teen the copy of second worksheet and pen or pencil. Explain that this is a match-up game to see how well the teen understands the ideas in the wheel of power and control. Together read each scenario and ask teen to draw a line to which type of controlling behavior the situation is an example of. Teen may refer to the Power & Control Wheel in order to complete the worksheet.
5. After teen has finished matching the examples to the behavior, provide the "answer key" and review each answer, explaining any mistakes.

Answer Key: (1) G (2) E (3) C (4) B (5) A (6) F (7) H (8) D

Use In Conjunction With:
SEALS II, *"Letting Go Of Other's Expectations,"* (page 74)
SEALS II, *"Letting Go of the Need to Control,"* (page 75)
SEALS III, *"It's Your Choice,"* (page 5)

Understanding Equality

The opposite of an abusive relationship (one based on power and control) is a healthy relationship, which is based on Equality. When both people in a relationship believe they are equal, and neither tries to gain power or control over the other, the result is a non-violent and healthy relationship. The 'Equality Wheel' below shows equality as the center of the healthy relationship. Inside the 'spokes' of the wheel are examples of behaviors that go on in a relationship based on equality.

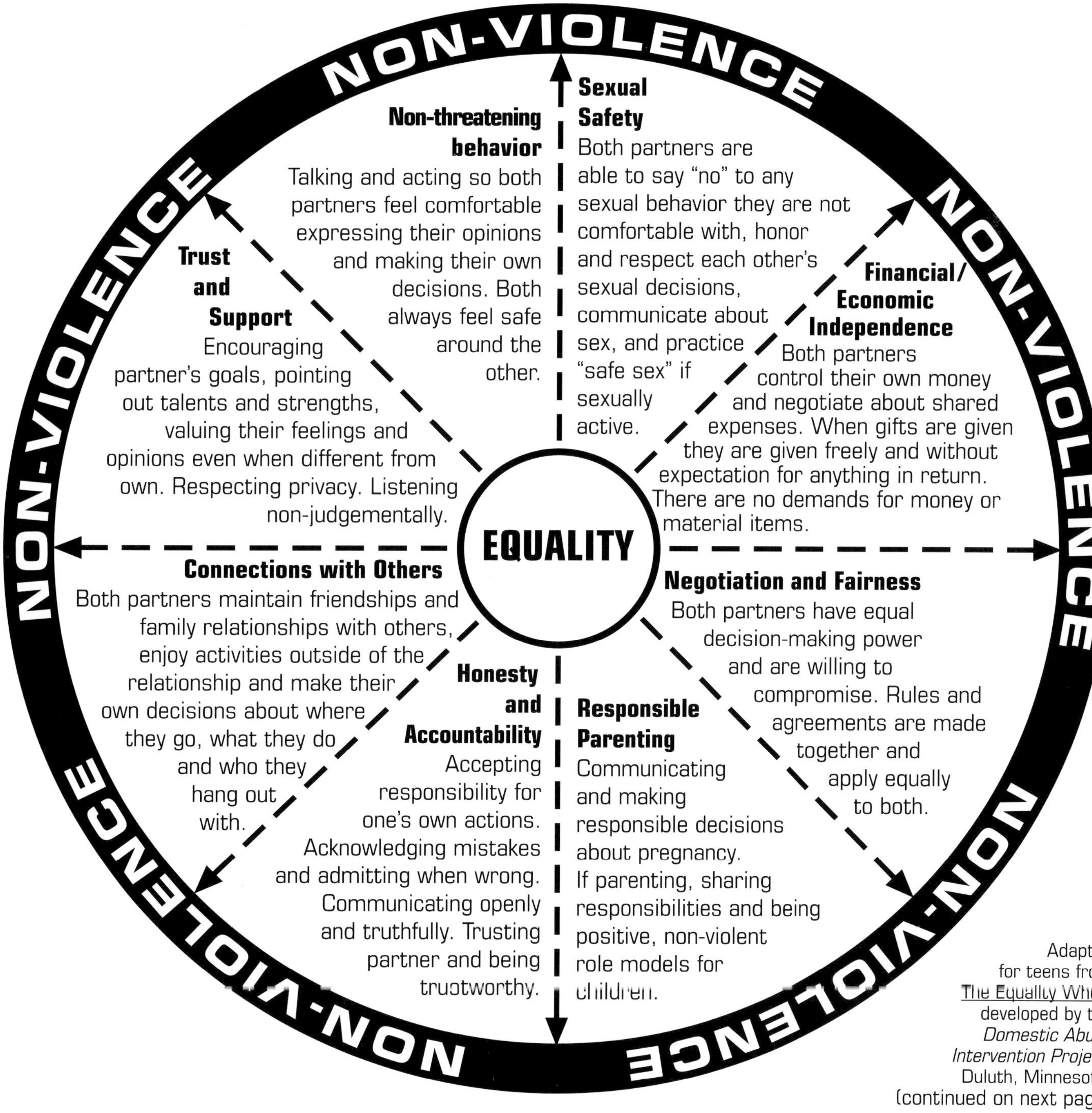

The Equality Wheel

Surrounding ring: **NON-VIOLENCE**

Center: **EQUALITY**

Non-threatening behavior
Talking and acting so both partners feel comfortable expressing their opinions and making their own decisions. Both always feel safe around the other.

Sexual Safety
Both partners are able to say "no" to any sexual behavior they are not comfortable with, honor and respect each other's sexual decisions, communicate about sex, and practice "safe sex" if sexually active.

Financial/Economic Independence
Both partners control their own money and negotiate about shared expenses. When gifts are given they are given freely and without expectation for anything in return. There are no demands for money or material items.

Negotiation and Fairness
Both partners have equal decision-making power and are willing to compromise. Rules and agreements are made together and apply equally to both.

Responsible Parenting
Communicating and making responsible decisions about pregnancy. If parenting, sharing responsibilities and being positive, non-violent role models for children.

Honesty and Accountability
Accepting responsibility for one's own actions. Acknowledging mistakes and admitting when wrong. Communicating openly and truthfully. Trusting partner and being trustworthy.

Connections with Others
Both partners maintain friendships and family relationships with others, enjoy activities outside of the relationship and make their own decisions about where they go, what they do and who they hang out with.

Trust and Support
Encouraging partner's goals, pointing out talents and strengths, valuing their feelings and opinions even when different from own. Respecting privacy. Listening non-judgementally.

Adapted for teens from The Equality Wheel developed by the *Domestic Abuse Intervention Project*, Duluth, Minnesota.
(continued on next page)

Understanding Equality (continued)

Each sentence below is an example of the behaviors described in the "Equality Wheel" on the previous page. Draw a line to match the examples on the left to the Equality Behaviors on the right.

1. Sarah is a member of a leadership group and has the chance to go on a week-long college tour with the guys and girls in the group. Her boyfriend Josh tells her he will miss her, but encourages her to go because he knows she wants to go to college and will have a good time traveling.

2. Chris and Armeen had a bad fight last night and Armeen punched a hole in the wall. Armeen apologizes and says Chris doesn't deserve to be treated that way. He agrees to see a counselor, and follows through with his promise.

3. Danny and Taria have a child together. Danny works at night so he can take care of the baby during the day while Taria is in school, and once a week they share the cost of a babysitter so they can take parenting classes.

4. When Natasha tells Dennis that the girls are getting together for a friend's birthday on Friday, Dennis says he will miss their regular date but encourages her to have a good time. Dennis makes plans to play ball with the guys.

5. When Cindy tells Adam she would like to take him out to dinner, she pays; Adam then offers to pay for the movie, and Cindy agrees to this.

6. Steven and Tia often argue. Even though Steven is twice Tia's size, he never uses his size or strength to intimidate her, and Tia is never afraid to say what she thinks. They respect each other's opinions and feelings.

7. On their third date, Ken wants to have sex but Karen isn't ready, so he doesn't pressure her. Although it's awkward, they discuss their feelings about sex. When they're both ready they go to the health center for HIV tests and birth control.

8. Lee wants to go to a movie tonight and Sam wants to go to a concert. They agree that since the concert is a one-time thing, they will go to that tonight and Sam will change his schedule around tomorrow so they can go to the movie together.

A. Honesty and Accountability

B. Sexual Safety

C. Trust and Support

D. Non-threatening Behavior

E. Responsible Parenting

F. Financial/Economic Independence

G. Connection with Others

H. Negotiation and Fairness

Facilitator's Information for
Understanding Equality

Purpose: To identify and understand some of the behaviors found in healthy relationships based on equality.

Materials: One photocopy of each worksheet per participant
Pens/pencils
Additional for GROUP: Additional photocopy of second worksheet, cut up into eight pieces of paper with one situation on each paper
Tape
Flipchart and markers/blackboard and chalk

Activity Group:
1. This activity should be done as a follow-up to Understanding Power & Control Tactics. Explain that this activity is about the opposite of a relationship based on power and control – it's about a healthy relationship, one based on equality.
2. Ahead of time, draw a large outline of the wheel on board or flipchart with the headings only for each section written in.
3. Distribute page one, the equality wheel. Review the wheel visually first, explaining that in the center is equality, because healthy relationships are based on a 50-50 partnership where both partners are equal. In between the 'spokes' of the wheel are the behaviors that support equality. On the outside of the wheel is non-violence. If people in a relationship believe both partners are equal and practice the behaviors inside the spokes of the equality wheel, it should lead to a completely non-violent relationship.
4. Review each section of the wheel, reading the heading and the examples listed on the worksheet. Ask group members if they can think of examples in their own lives, in the lives of people they know, or in TV shows or movies.
5. Pass out pieces of paper with scenarios from page two. If you have more than 8 group members you can make up additional examples, or just ask for 8 group members to volunteer.
6. Ask each group member with a paper to read his or her scenario aloud, decide where on the wheel that example falls and tape the piece of paper on the large wheel. Ask the rest of the group if they agree, and if not, where they think it should go.
7. Repeat this with each scenario until there is an example taped to each section of the wheel. Provide the "answer key" and review answers.
8. Distribute photocopies of page two and instruct teens to draw a line from each scenario to the behavior it represents.

Activity Individual:
1. This activity should be done as a follow-up to Understanding Power & Control Tactics. Explain that this activity is about the opposite of a relationship based on power and control – it's about a healthy relationship, one based on equality.
2. Give teen page one, the equality wheel, and read or have teen read the introductory paragraph.
3. Review the wheel visually first, explaining that the center is equality, because healthy relationships are based on a 50-50 partnership where both partners are equal. In between the 'spokes' of the wheel are the behaviors that support equality. On the outside of the wheel is non-violence. If people in a relationship believe both partners are equal and practice the behaviors inside the spokes of the equality wheel, it should lead to a completely non-violent relationship.
4. Review each section of the wheel, first reading the examples listed and then asking the teen if s/he can think of any examples in his/her life, in the lives of people s/he knows, or in TV shows or movies.
5. After reviewing the wheel, give teen page two and a pen or pencil. Explain that this is a match-up game to see how well the teen understands the ideas in the equality wheel. Together read each scenario, and ask teen to draw a line from each scenario to the example it represents.
6. After teen has finished matching the examples to the behavior, provide the 'answer key' and review each answer, explaining any mistakes.

Answer Key: (1) C (2) A (3) E (4) G (5) F (6) D (7) B (8) H

Use In Conjunction With:
SEALS+PLUS, *"What Are Your Lifesavers,"* (page 62)
SEALS II, *"Deepening Relationships,"* (page 38)
SEALS III, *"Setting Boundaries,"* (page 52)
CROSSING THE BRIDGE, (pages 49, 50, 51)

Focus on Emotional Abuse

Emotional abuse is a way of hurting someone without necessarily being physical. It's when one person in a relationship tries to control the other person's feelings or thoughts in order to gain power over them.

I am evaluating my relationship with: _____

Some examples of emotional abuse (also called mental, verbal or psychological abuse) are listed below. Check any that you have done to this person, or that this person has done to you.

	I have done to this person	They have done to me
Put-downs; Calling names, telling them they're stupid or ugly, telling them they're not good enough or no one could ever love them	☐	☐
Frequently cursing or yelling at the other person	☐	☐
Threatening or intimidating - making the other person feel nervous or scared for themselves or someone they care about	☐	☐
Frequently criticizing or correcting the other person - the way they look, talk, act, etc.	☐	☐
Lying or cheating	☐	☐
Playing mind games or making the other person think they're crazy	☐	☐
Putting responsibility for your behavior on the other person	☐	☐
Making fun of or putting down the other person's family, culture, religion, race or heritage	☐	☐
Embarrassing or humiliating the other person, especially in front of other people	☐	☐
Withholding affection as punishment - not giving them love if they don't do what you want them to do	☐	☐
Controlling behavior - telling the other person what to do, what to wear, who to hang out with, etc.	☐	☐
Making all the decisions in the relationship and ignoring the other person's feelings	☐	☐
Guilt trips - trying to make the other person feel guilty when you don't get your way, especially by threatening to hurt yourself or commit suicide	☐	☐
Keeping the other person from spending time with their friends or family members, or from work or other activities that are important to him/her	☐	☐
Using the children to get the other person to do what you want	☐	☐
Being extremely jealous, and using jealousy to justify controlling behavior	☐	☐
Threatening to break up with the other person if you don't get your way	☐	☐
Saying you don't love the other person just to get him/her to do what you want	☐	☐
Accusing the other person of cheating on you as a way of manipulating him/her to do what you want	☐	☐
Keeping constant tabs on a person, expecting to know his/her every move	☐	☐

Here are some examples of emotional abuse I have experienced in my life (not necessarily from the person above):

_____

_____

CHECKPOINT:
Am I being emotionally abused by my partner? __ Yes __ No
Have I been emotionally abused in the past? __ Yes __ No
Am I being emotionally abusive to my partner? __ Yes __ No
Have I been emotionally abusive in the past? __ Yes __ No

Facilitator's Information for
Focus on Emotional Abuse

Purpose: To develop a deeper understanding of the meaning of emotional abuse, and identify instances when participant(s) have been emotionally abused or abusive.

Materials: One photocopy of worksheet per participant
Pens/pencils

Activity (Group or Individual):
1. Distribute worksheet(s) and read or have a participant volunteer to read aloud the introductory paragraph.
2. Ask teen(s) if they think that every time someone gets their feelings hurt in a relationship, it means someone is being abusive. Ask for examples of how feelings get hurt in a non-abusive relationship, and acknowledge that hurt feelings occur in all relationships.
3. Instruct teen(s) to identify the relationship they will evaluate, and write the person's name in the box if they are comfortable doing so.
4. Read or have participant(s) read aloud each example of emotionally abusive behavior. Instruct teen(s) to check any type of emotional abuse they have experienced, and invite group members to share examples if they wish.
5. After completing the list, ask participant(s) to think about one specific example of emotional abuse they have experienced, not necessarily by the person in the relationship they evaluated above. Stress that while everyone may not have been in a relationship where there was a pattern of one person controlling the other, everyone has manipulated another person or been manipulated before. Instruct participant(s) to write one such example in the space provided.
6. If working with a group, invite participant(s) to share with the group an example of emotional abuse they have experienced (as abuser or abused).
7. Ask the participant(s) to decide for themselves whether they think they are or have been emotionally abused or abusive, and check the appropriate boxes at the bottom of the page.

Use In Conjunction With:
SEALS+PLUS, *"Emotions,"* (page 24)
SEALS II, *"Deepening Relationships,"* (page 38)
SEALS III, *"Sticks & Stones,"* (page 53)
CROSSING THE BRIDGE, (pages 12, 28, 29, 30, 31)

Case Study: Emotional Abuse

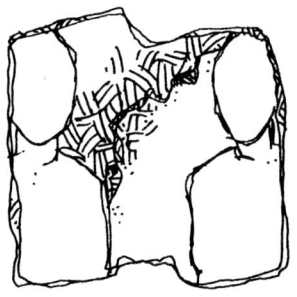

Maria and James*

Seventeen-year-old Maria came to counseling confused about whether she was treating her boyfriend fairly — he told her she was being emotionally abusive. She had been going out with James for about a year, and was not willing to have sex with him. He said she was being selfish and didn't care about his needs. He told her that her decision to remain a virgin was eventually going to force him to break up with her.

As Maria and her counselor talked, she described some things James had done to hurt her feelings. When she wrote him a letter telling him how much she loves him, he corrected her spelling and grammar mistakes in red pen on the letter, then gave it back to her and told her he would accept the letter after she made the corrections. Maria told her counselor that James often corrects the way she talks and writes, but he says he does this because he loves her and wants to help her become a better person. The other day in the cafeteria he snapped at her for using slang, then told his friends that her parents are immigrants and can't speak English, so since she can't learn anything from them, he has to teach her.

Names and identifying information have been changed.

Which examples of emotional abuse listed on the Focus on Emotional Abuse page are described in this story?

1. _____
2. _____
3. _____
4. _____
5. _____

Around the issue of whether or not to have sex, who is being abusive, James or Maria? Why?
_____
_____

How do you think Maria felt when James gave her letter back with corrections on it?
_____

How is James justifying his behavior?
_____
_____

How is James manipulating Maria?
_____
_____

Do you think James realizes he is being emotionally abusive? Why or why not?
_____
_____

What advice would you give to Maria?
_____
_____

Facilitator's Information for
Case Study: Emotional Abuse

Purpose: To apply knowledge about emotional abuse to a case study in order to better understand the dynamics of emotional abuse.

Materials: One photocopy of worksheet per participant
Pens/pencils
Copies of completed worksheets Focus on Emotional Abuse

Activity (Group or Individual):
1. Hand out copies of Focus on Emotional Abuse and briefly review activity.
2. Tell participant(s) that this new activity is going to build on the knowledge they gained in the last activity, Focus on Emotional Abuse.
3. Hand out worksheet Case Study: Emotional Abuse.
4. Read or have participant(s) read aloud Maria and James' story.
5. Instruct participant(s) to answer questions about Maria and James' story individually, allowing about ten minutes to do so. Tell participant(s) that they can use the Focus on Emotional Abuse worksheet to refer to.
6. After participant(s) have completed worksheet, review answers. Be sure that the following points are addressed:
   * Examples of emotional abuse from Focus on Emotional Abuse include James manipulating Maria into feeling responsible for his choices or actions, frequently criticizing/correcting her, putting down her family, embarrassing/humiliating her, guilt trips, threatening to break up.
   * A person always has the right to make his or her own decisions about whether or not to have sex. Making a decision that's healthy for yourself does not mean you are not being considerate of the other person - it just means you are not willing to put the other person above yourself.
   * Sex is not a 'need.' It is a 'want.'
   * By saying he will be forced to break up with her, James is putting responsibility for his choices on Maria. It is his decision whether or not to stay in a relationship that doesn't include sexual intercourse.
   * James justifies his behavior by saying he wants to make Maria a 'better person.' This is a common justification for abuse. He is not her parent or her teacher, and he is not responsible for teaching her. If she asks for help with homework that is one thing - but by correcting her letters and her speech in public, he is only embarrassing her and making her feel badly about herself.
   * James may or may not consciously realize how he is hurting and manipulating Maria, but on some level he is doing it to gain power and control over her. Whether it's conscious or not, James' behavior is his responsibility.
   * If she is not ready to end the relationship, Maria can work on being assertive and setting limits (see activities on these issues.) She can clearly tell James how she feels about his behavior, and insist he stop. She can stand her ground on the issue of sex and tell him clearly that she will not be pressured. She can make decisions about her own limits in terms of the relationship, and at what point she will end the relationship if James continues to be emotionally abusive.

Use In Conjunction With:
SEALS+PLUS, *"Lighten Up,"* (page 18)
SEALS II, *"Passive Aggressive,"* (page 7)
SEALS III, *"Sticks & Stones,"* (page 53)

Focus on Physical Abuse

Physical abuse is any behavior that is meant to cause hurt to another person's body or to control another person's physical freedom or movement. One person may abuse another using his or her own physical strength, using an object or weapon, or using size or presence to intimidate or control the other.

I am evaluating my relationship with: _____

Some examples of physical abuse are below.
Check any that you have done to this person or they have done to you.

	I have done to this person	This person has done to me
Pushing or shoving	☐	☐
Grabbing	☐	☐
Hitting, slapping or punching	☐	☐
Pulling hair	☐	☐
Kicking	☐	☐
Choking	☐	☐
Holding someone down or holding their arm so they can't walk away	☐	☐
Throwing objects at another person	☐	☐
Use of weapons to hurt or threaten someone	☐	☐
Biting	☐	☐
Pinching	☐	☐
Spitting	☐	☐
Arm twisting	☐	☐
Burning	☐	☐
Carrying someone against their will	☐	☐
Trapping someone in a room or car	☐	☐
Abandoning someone in an unsafe place	☐	☐
Chasing	☐	☐
Standing in the doorway to block the other person from leaving	☐	☐
Hiding car keys, shoes, clothes or money so the other person can't leave	☐	☐
Standing in front of/behind car to prevent person from leaving	☐	☐
Sabotaging car to prevent person from leaving	☐	☐
Refusing to help someone when they're sick or injured	☐	☐
Following or stalking	☐	☐

Here are some examples of physical abuse I have experienced in my life (not necessarily from the person above):

_____

_____

CHECKPOINT:
Am I being physically abused by my partner? __ Yes __ No
Have I been physically abused in the past? __ Yes __ No
Am I being physically abusive to my partner? __ Yes __ No
Have I been physically abusive in the past? __ Yes __ No

Facilitator's Information for
Focus on Physical Abuse

Purpose: To develop a deeper understanding of the meaning of physical abuse.
To identify instances when participants have been physically abused or abusive.

Materials: One photocopy of worksheet per participant
Pens/pencils

Optional: Flip chart and markers/blackboard and chalk

Activity (Group):
1. Introduce activity by stating that today the group is going to focus on one of the forms of abuse, physical abuse.
2. As one group or in several smaller groups, ask teens to brainstorm as many specific examples of physical abuse as they can. Explain that by specific, you mean a single action - instead of 'beating', break it down to 'punching,' 'slapping,' 'kicking.' Give each group a piece of large paper or space on the blackboard to make its lists.
3. Give group(s) about ten minutes to make its lists.
4. If activity is done in more than one group, reconvene the larger group and ask each workgroup to read and explain its list to the larger group. After each group has reviewed its list, note any similarities and differences in the lists.
5. Distribute worksheets and read or have a participant volunteer to read aloud the introductory paragraph.
6. Instruct participants to identify a relationship they will evaluate, and write the person's name in the box if they are comfortable doing so.
7. Read or have participants read aloud each example of physically abusive behavior. Instruct participants who are comfortable doing so to check any type of physical abuse they have experienced. Facilitator may invite group members to share examples if they wish, and guide the group in offering support.
8. After completing the list, ask teens to think about one specific example of physical abuse they have experienced, not necessarily by the person in the relationship they evaluated above. Stress that while everyone may not have been in a relationship where there was a pattern of one person physically abusing the other, many people have experienced at least one of the more subtle forms of physical abuse by a partner, peer or family member. (Give examples of being trapped in a room or car, being smacked by a peer, etc.) Ask participants to write one such example in the space provided.
9. Ask the teens to decide for themselves whether they think they are or have been physically abused or abusive, and check the appropriate boxes at the bottom of the page.
10. Process whether participants have learned anything new from this activity, whether anyone has realized for the first time that they have been involved in a physically abusive relationship and what that feels like, and if so, what steps need to be taken based on this realization.

Activity (Individual):
1. Give teen worksheet and read or have teen read aloud the introductory paragraph.
2. Acknowledge that talking or even thinking about physical abuse can be very difficult. Discuss the participant's comfort level with learning about the different types of abuse. Allow teen to decide whether s/he wants to participate by completing the checklist based on a personal relationship, or just learn about what the different types of abuse are without applying it to him/herself at this time.
3. Read or have participant read each example of physically abusive behavior, and discuss examples in his or her life or hypothetical examples. Instruct teen to check any type of physical abuse he or she has experienced, if comfortable doing so.
4. After completing the list, ask participant to think about one specific example of physical abuse s/he has experienced and write the example in the space provided.
5. Ask the participant to decide for him/herself whether s/he is or has been physically abused or abusive, and check the appropriate boxes at the bottom of the page.
6. Process whether teen realized anything new about his or her experiences, how that feels and whether s/he wants to make changes based on this realization.

Use In Conjunction With:
SEALS+PLUS, *"I Have The Right to Change a Situation,"* (page 12)
SEALS II, *"Journal Keeping,"* (page 16)
SEALS III, *"My Play,"* (page 62)

Focus on Sexual Abuse

Sexual abuse is any sexual behavior that is forced, coerced or manipulated. It includes sexual harassment, which is discussed in more detail in the separate worksheet <u>Focus on Sexual Harassment</u>. Sexual abuse overlaps with the other types of abuse, because it can be physical (such as unwanted touching), verbal (such as calling someone sexual names) or emotional (such as using sexual behavior to humiliate someone.)

Some examples of sexual abuse are listed below.
Check any that you have ever done to someone or someone else has done to you.

	I have done	Have had done to me
▷ Threatening to break up with someone or spread rumors about them if they refuse sexual acts	☐	☐
▷ Threatening to hurt the other person or someone they care about if they refuse sexual acts	☐	☐
▷ Lying to or manipulating someone to get him/her to agree to sexual behavior	☐	☐
▷ Ripping or tearing at someone's clothes	☐	☐
▷ Unwanted grabbing or touching of someone's rear end, breasts, or genital areas	☐	☐
▷ Forcing someone to take off his/her clothes	☐	☐
▷ Physically forcing someone into any kind of sexual behavior – even when they have agreed to one form of sex but not to another	☐	☐
▷ Sex while one person is too drunk or high to make a sound decision about sex	☐	☐
▷ Forcing someone into sexual acts with a third person	☐	☐
▷ Forcing someone to watch sex between others	☐	☐
▷ Taking pictures or videos of someone undressing or involved in sexual behavior without his/her consent	☐	☐
▷ Any sexual activity between an adult and child or a child and a much younger child	☐	☐
▷ Rape with an object	☐	☐
▷ Sex that hurts	☐	☐
▷ Withholding sex as a way of manipulating someone into doing what you want	☐	☐
▷ Making partner dress in a sexier way or less sexy way	☐	☐
▷ Sexual harassment (see <u>Focus on Sexual Harassment</u> for details on this form of sexual abuse.)	☐	☐
▷ _____	☐	☐
▷ _____	☐	☐

Here are some examples of sexual abuse I have experienced:

_____
_____

CHECKPOINT:
Am I being sexually abused by my partner? __ Yes __ No
Have I been sexually abused in the past? __ Yes __ No
Am I being sexually abusive to my partner? __ Yes __ No
Have I been sexually abusive in the past? __ Yes __ No

Facilitator's Information for
Focus on Sexual Abuse

Purpose: To develop a deeper understanding of the meaning of sexual abuse.
To identify instances when participants have been sexually abused or abusive.

Materials: One photocopy of worksheet per participant
Pens/pencils

Activity (Group or Individual):

1. Distribute worksheet(s) and read or have a participant(s) read aloud the introductory paragraph.
2. Acknowledge that talking or even thinking about sexual abuse can be very difficult and painful for people who have experienced it.
   * In an individual session, discuss the participant's comfort level with learning about the different types of abuse and allow him/her to decide whether s/he wants to participate by completing the checklist, or just learn about what the different types of abuse are without applying it to him/herself.
   * In a group setting, tell the group that you would like everyone to at least learn about the many different types of sexual abuse so they can identify them in the future. Give group members the individual option of completing the checklist or not without asking them to state their choice for the group. Emphasize that no one should feel pressured to talk about any experience they are not comfortable talking about. Reiterate group agreements around confidentiality and mutual support.
3. Read or have participant(s) read each example of sexually abusive behavior. Instruct participants, who are comfortable doing so, to check any type of sexual abuse they have experienced. If appropriate, invite group members to share examples if they wish, and guide the group in offering support.
4. After completing the list, ask participant(s) to think about one specific example of sexual abuse they have experienced. Stress that while not everyone may have been in a relationship where there was a pattern of one person sexually abusing the other, most people, especially females, have experienced at least one of the more subtle forms of sexual abuse. (Give examples of being called a sexual name or being hassled on the street.) Invite participants, if they are comfortable, to write one such example in the space provided.
5. Ask participant(s) to decide for themselves whether they think they are or have been sexually abused or abusive, and check the appropriate boxes at the bottom of the page.
6. Process whether participant(s) have learned anything new from this activity, whether anyone has realized for the first time that they have been involved in a sexually abusive relationship and what that feels like, and if so, what steps need to be taken based on this realization.

Note to facilitator: Because this activity asks participant(s) to identify instances of sexual abuse, it should only be done in groups or therapeutic relationships where there is a strong sense of trust and intimacy. It is very important that the professional be prepared to offer support and clinical intervention for a participant who discloses sexual abuse.

Use In Conjunction With:
SEALS+PLUS, *"Significant Life Events,"* (page 28)
SEALS II, *"We Are People With...,"* (page 8)
SEALS III, *"Coping Tree,"* (page 1)

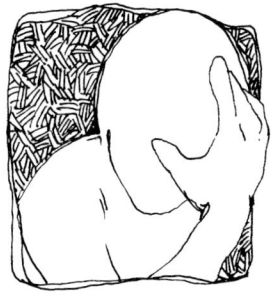

Painful Memory

The following poem, written by a student in the Bronx, New York, describes circumstances and feelings that are very common to date rape. After reading the poem, use the space on the right to either (A) write your own poem about sexual abuse, or (B) write down the feelings and thoughts this poem brings up in you.

PAINFUL MEMORY
By Amanda D.

1. I remember that day clearly,
   as if it was just yesterday,
   and I guess it's because it's a painful memory
   that can never go away.

2. You said that I could trust you -
   only to the movies we would go.
   Something much more dangerous was coming,
   but that I didn't know.

3. It was only when I pointed out
   that you were driving me home the wrong way,
   "I have a special treat for you"
   was all to me you'd say.

4. Innocent and defenseless as I was,
   intuition persisted now.
   You said things that touched my heart,
   and I thought, "How can I leave him now?"

5. You parked the car in the driveway
   and told me your parents weren't home,
   and that you need someone to talk to
   of your depression and how you were feeling alone.

6. Even though I felt awkward,
   I still followed you inside.
   We did talk about you
   but that subject soon declined.

7. First you told me sweet things,
   and started to touch my hair,
   then you put your arms around me
   and said I was the only one who cared.

8. One thing led to another
   and soon your body stood naked before mine.
   You saw my hesitation and said everything would be fine.

9. You took my hand softly
   And led me to the bed.
   With your body so close to mine
   I made a gesture, and there a tear I shed.

10. Before we even started,
    I felt my conscience telling me this was wrong.
    I knew I must speak up,
    'cause I knew it would be too late if I took too long.

11. I told you I couldn't do it.
    You stood, eyes open and mouth wide
    You still moved a little closer
    but I moved over to the other side.

12. You still came closer,
    and next to the wall I was trapped.
    You tried to change my mind by kissing me,
    and your arms around me you wrapped.

13. I pushed you away
    and told you my answer was "NO!"
    But you grabbed hold of my wrist
    and said "We're still gonna do it, 'hoe."

14. I tried to fight you off me
    but you were man and you were strong.
    In a sweet voice you said,
    "Don't worry honey, this won't take long."

15. After you were through,
    I felt dirty and ashamed.
    You were controlling me,
    Like a man whose lion he tames.

16. I stood there in disbelief,
    knowing you had committed rape.
    It's the feeling I've been marked with ever since with you, I thought I was safe.

Facilitator's Information for
Painful Memory

Purpose: To recognize circumstances common to date rape.
To recognize and empathize with feelings common among victims of date rape.

Materials: One photocopy of worksheet per participant
Pens/pencils

Activity (Group or Individual):
1. Introduce activity by reviewing any previous discussion about rape and stating that this is a poem about date rape written by a high school student.
2. Read or have a participant read the poem aloud.
3. Instruct participant(s) to take ten minutes to write down any feelings or thoughts the poem brought up in them, or to write their own poem about sexual abuse. Allow extra time if needed.
4. Ask participant(s) if anyone would like to share their poem or thoughts with the group, and process as necessary. Be sure to include discussion of the date rape dynamics discussed in the poem that are listed below.
5. Ask participant(s) how writing, whether it be poetry or just writing down feelings, might help a person who has been through a difficult experience like rape to work out their "painful memories." Encourage participant(s) to write poetry, fiction or prose or to journal regularly to work through their own thoughts and feelings about relationships.

Alternate Activity (Group or Individual):
1. Introduce activity by reviewing previous discussion about rape and stating that this is a poem about date rape written by a high school student. Read or have a participant read the poem aloud.
2. State that every stanza (paragraph) in this poem makes a point about the dynamics of date rape by giving an example of a circumstance or feeling that is common to date rape. (Review the meaning of the term "dynamics" if necessary.)
3. With participant(s), go through the poem reading one stanza at a time and prompting participant(s) to point out the dynamic that the author is giving an example of. Following are suggested discussion points for each stanza.

Stanza 1:	Rape has long-lasting emotional effects. (However, there is help to work through the emotions.)
Stanza 2:	Rapists are usually someone who the victim trusts.
Stanza 3:	Rapists often manipulate their victims in order to get them alone.
Stanza 4:	People often do not trust their intuition because the rapist is so charming and manipulative. (It is very important to trust your gut if you are uncomfortable with a person!)
Stanza 5:	Most rapes take place in the home or car of the victim or offender. (Again, the young man in this example manipulates the young woman into going to his house by saying he needed someone to talk to.)
Stanza 6:	Again, it is very important to go with your gut - however in this example, the young woman was manipulated into going inside with her date.
Stanza 7:	Another example of how the young man manipulates the young woman by making her feel good and getting her to trust him.
Stanza 8:	One warning sign of an abusive person is someone who doesn't respect your feelings. Even though the young man saw that the young woman was uncomfortable with the situation, he continued to pressure her.
Stanza 9:	Sexual abusers often start out sweet and gentle - it is only when they don't get what they want that they get aggressive.
Stanza 10:	Assertiveness (speaking up clearly for yourself) is very important in protecting yourself from abuse.
Stanza 11:	Another example of the young man not respecting the young woman's feelings - when she told him no the first time, he didn't respect that and continued to try to persuade her.
Stanza 12:	Here the young man continues to try to pressure the young woman into sexual activity.
Stanza 13:	When an abuser's emotional tactics don't work to control his partner, he might suddenly "turn mean" and get physically and verbally aggressive.
Stanza 14:	In most cases, men have greater physical strength than women, and abusive men will use this strength to gain power and control.
Stanza 15:	Feelings of shame, guilt and being "dirty" are normal after rape - however the victim of rape has NOTHING to be ashamed or guilty about because she has done nothing wrong. As the poem says, the rapist was the one in control, and he is the one who is in the wrong.
Stanza 16:	Shock and disbelief are also common feelings after rape, especially with someone the victim trusted or felt safe with. These feelings need to be worked through with a counselor/therapist.

Use In Conjunction With:
SEALS II, *"What Have I Been Up To?,"* (page 18)
SEALS II, *"Write To Heal,"* (page 19)
SEALS II, *"Poetry Power,"* (page 20)

Focus on Sexual Harassment

Sexual Harassment is any unwanted sexual attention that makes a person feel threatened, uncomfortable or unsafe. Often, but not always, the harasser has some kind of power over the person they are harassing – for example a boss. Males and females can be sexually harassed.

Some examples of sexual harassment are listed below.
Check any that you have ever done to someone or someone has done to you.

	I have done	Have had done to me

Physical forms of sexual harassment:
- Unwanted touching, grabbing or pinching someone's rear end, breasts or genital areas ☐ ☐
- 'Accidentally' brushing up against someone ☐ ☐
- Any unwanted touching of a sexual nature, such as caressing someone's hair or face ☐ ☐
- Kissing someone when they don't want to be kissed ☐ ☐
- Standing in someone's way while verbally or non-verbally harassing them ☐ ☐
- Other: _____ ☐ ☐

Verbal forms of sexual harassment:
- Pressure to go out on a date or engage in sexual activity ☐ ☐
- Comments about a person's body that make them feel uncomfortable ☐ ☐
- Making jokes of a sexual nature that make another person uncomfortable – even if the jokes are not told to the person directly, but they are meant to 'overhear' ☐ ☐
- Jokes that put down members of the opposite sex ☐ ☐
- Spreading sexual rumors about a person ☐ ☐
- Names or words that belittle someone's gender or sexual orientation ☐ ☐
- 'Dirty' notes or letters ☐ ☐
- Sexual noises or whistles ☐ ☐
- Obscene prank phone calls ☐ ☐
- Threatening (or implying) that a person's job will be affected by refusing or agreeing to be sexually involved with an employer, co-worker or other person in the workplace ☐ ☐
- Threatening (or implying) that a student's grades or school performance will be affected by refusing or agreeing to be sexually involved with a teacher, school administrator or other person in the school ☐ ☐
- Other: _____ ☐ ☐

Nonverbal forms of sexual harassment:
- Sexual drawings, nude or 'sexy' posters that make a person uncomfortable in the school or workplace ☐ ☐
- Staring at someone's body parts in a way that makes them uncomfortable ☐ ☐
- Gestures or expressions that are meant to be sexual – for example, licking lips or 'pantomiming' sexual behavior ☐ ☐
- Other: _____ ☐ ☐

If you are ever unsure about whether what you are doing is sexual harassment, think about this: Would you want someone doing the same thing to your child, brother, sister or parent?

CHECKPOINT:
Am I being sexually harassed by anyone now?	__ Yes __ No
Have I been sexually harassed in the past?	__ Yes __ No
Am I sexually harassing anyone now?	__ Yes __ No
Have I sexually harassed anyone in the past?	__ Yes __ No

(continued on next page)

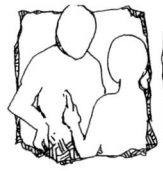

Focus on Sexual Harassment

(continued)

WHAT TO DO IF YOU ARE BEING SEXUALLY HARASSED

If you are experiencing sexual harassment, the sooner you address it the easier it will be to deal with. Many victims of sexual harassment try to ignore it because it is embarrassing, they want to get along with people or they are afraid of what the harasser will do. But if you let it go, the harasser might get the message that his or her behavior is okay with you and it could get out of control. Below are some steps you can take to address sexual harassment.

1. Make it very clear to the person harassing you that you want it to STOP immediately. Use assertive words to let him or her know that you are not comfortable with the behavior. Tell them you feel harassed. Do not laugh or smile at them.
   Write what you will say to your harasser here: _____
   _____

2. Keep a log. Write down everything that happens – the names, places, times, exactly what was said or done, and the names of any witnesses.
   Start by writing how your harassment began, and attach extra pages if necessary. (The more detailed the better)
   Date: _____ Name(s) of people involved: _____
   What was said or done: _____
   _____
   How you responded: _____
   Any witnesses or people you told about the incident: _____

3. Tell someone in a position of authority. If you are at school, tell a teacher or guidance counselor you trust. If you are at work, tell a supervisor. If the problem continues and the person in authority doesn't do anything, tell someone higher up.
   Who will you tell? _____
   Once you have told this person, write their response here: _____
   Also write the responses of people you tell in your log.

4. Try not to be alone with the harasser. You might be able to get friends or co-workers to help by sticking close. What friends or co-workers will you ask for help? _____

5. File a complaint and get advice from experts in the area of sexual harassment. Write in the number for your state's division of human rights/sexual harassment unit or other place you will call: _____

6. Get help in taking care of yourself emotionally. People who are sexually harassed often feel violated, embarrassed, ashamed, angry and confused. All of these feelings are normal, but it is important to get help working through them. Write the name of a counselor or other adult who you can confide in. _____

7. Remember, Sexual Harassment is NOT your fault. It is another example of abuse, when someone is trying to gain power and control over another person.

Write A Sexual Harassment Role-Play Here

Characters:

The Harassment:

What the person being harassed does in response:

Facilitator's Information for
Focus on Sexual Harassment

Purpose: To define sexual harassment and identify different forms of sexual harassment.
To know what to do if one is being sexually harassed.

Materials: One photocopy of each worksheet per participant
Pens/pencils
Phone number(s) for local/state sexual harassment help lines. Look in the phone book for the state division of human rights' sexual harassment unit, the local Equal Employment Opportunity Commission, or call the Department of Labor or a domestic violence hotline for information.

Activity (Group or Individual):
1. Distribute first page, Focus on Sexual Harassment and read or have participant(s) read aloud the introductory paragraph. Ask participant(s) if they can think of any examples where they have heard of people being sexually harassed in the news or on TV, etc., and discuss.
2. Read or have participant(s) read each of the examples under the different forms of sexual harassment. Discuss and prompt participant(s) to come up with examples for each one. Instruct participant(s) to check the boxes if they have been sexually harassed or if they have harassed someone else in any of the ways listed.
3. Read or have participant(s) read aloud the sentence "If you are ever unsure..." and discuss.
4. Instruct participant(s) to complete the questions under 'Checkpoint.'
5. Distribute second page, What to Do if You are Being Sexually Harassed and pens or pencils.
6. Tell participant(s) that if they checked the box on the last page saying they are being sexually harassed, they should complete this worksheet as an action plan for dealing with the harassment. People who are not being sexually harassed can still complete the worksheet based on what they will do if they ever find themselves in that position in the future. As an alternative, facilitator may read a story or show a video of a person being harassed and ask participant(s) to complete the worksheet as a plan for what the character in the story should do.
7. Read the introductory paragraph, and read or have participant(s) read aloud each of the questions. Allow time for participant(s) to fill in their answers in the space provided.
8. **If working with a group**, break participants up into groups of two or three and instruct them to develop a role-play where one person is sexually harassing the other. The person being harassed should use some of the suggestions in the worksheet to deal with the harassment. A third person can act as someone encouraging the harasser, someone helping the person being harassed, or the boss or teacher they will inform of the harassment. Instruct participants to write the scenario in the box provided, and then allow each group to perform their role-plays for the larger group.
If working with an individual, work with the teen to develop and write a scenario in which someone is being sexually harassed. The teen should role-play the part of the person being harassed, using some of the strategies in the worksheet.
9. Process with the following questions:
   * What are some of the reasons a person sexually harasses another? (To gain power and control, to humiliate them, to show off for friends, not being able to take no for an answer, thinking they are funny and being insensitive to how their jokes make others feel, etc.)
   * How do you think sexual harassment makes the person being harassed feel? (Embarrassed, helpless, afraid, angry, ashamed, guilty, confused about whether they are doing something to ask for it, etc.)
   * What are some of the excuses people use to justify sexual harassment? (S/he was flirting with me, liked it, dresses provocatively, brought it on with his/her sexual behavior, led me on, I was just joking, didn't mean anything by it, didn't know s/he didn't like it, etc.)
   * Has anyone ever laughed or smiled at someone when they were really uncomfortable? (This is normal, but it is a non-assertive behavior that others might take as meaning their behavior is OK. Discuss alternate assertive responses.)
   * After doing this activity, has anyone realized they have been sexually harassed or sexually harassed someone else, and not even realized it?
   * What is the difference between sexual harassment and flirting? (Flirting is when both people engage in the behavior, enjoy it, feel no pressure, and have equal power.)
   * Do guys get sexually harassed? (Yes) How is the pressure on a male being sexually harassed similar and different from the pressure on a female? (If a female harasses a male, the male is given the message he is supposed to like it and want sex under any circumstances. If harassed by a man, others might make fun of him and question his sexual orientation. When a gay male is harassed by another gay male, it brings-up stigmas and stereotypes about gays being 'perverts' that might make the victim even more hesitant to disclose. However, sexual harassment is equally painful for male and female victims.)

Use In Conjunction With:
SEALS+PLUS, *"I Have The Right To Change A Situation,"* (page 12)
SEALS II, *"Awareness Journal,"* (page 52)
SEALS III, *"Talking About Personal Issues,"* (page 54)

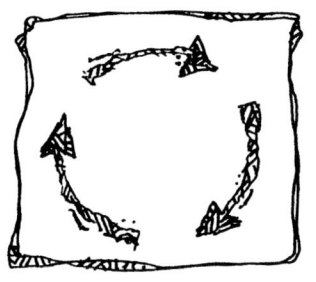 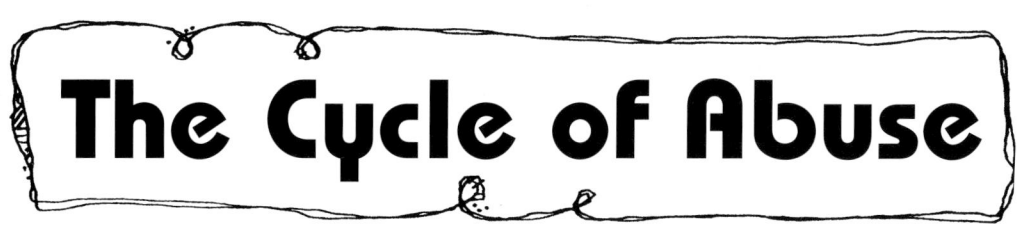

The Cycle of Abuse

Although not all abusive relationships follow the same pattern, there is a cycle that is similar in many abusive relationships. It looks something like this.

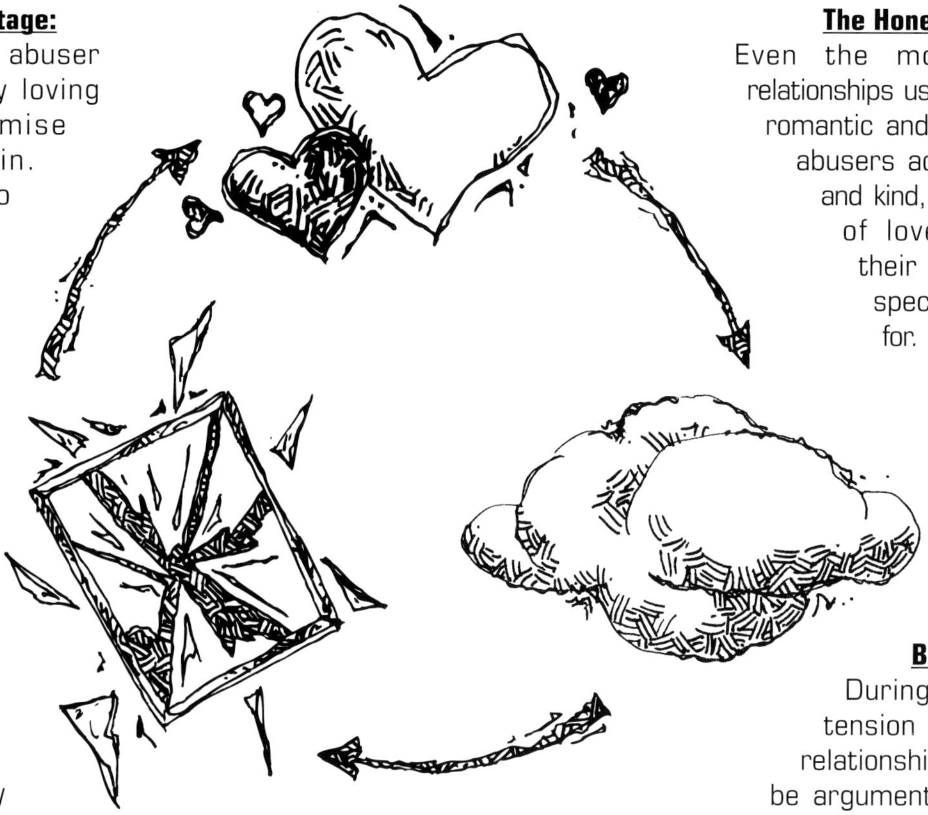

Back to The Honeymoon Stage:
After the 'blow up' the abuser may apologize, be very loving and kind, and promise it won't happen again. Because the abuser is so convincing, the partner will often try to 'forgive and forget.' Unfortunately, the cycle usually repeats itself and the abuse gets worse.

The Honeymoon Stage:
Even the most abusive relationships usually start out romantic and loving. Many abusers act very sweet and kind, express a lot of love and make their partners feel special and cared for.

The Blow Up Stage:
This is when the abuse is at its worst, and it may include extreme physical or sexual violence.

The Tension Building Stage:
During this phase, tension builds in the relationship. There may be arguments, emotional abuse or minor physical abuse like grabbing or pushing.

Have you experienced this cycle in your relationship? If so, briefly write down the behaviors you saw during each of the phases. Or think of a relationship from a movie, book or TV, and write down examples of behaviors you saw at each stage of the relationship.

1. The Honeymoon Stage (beginning of the relationship): _____

2. The Tension Building Stage: _____

3. The Blow Up Stage: _____

4. The Honeymoon Stage (after the blow up): _____

Facilitator's Information for
The Cycle of Abuse

Purpose: To understand and identify the 'Honeymoon,' 'Tension Building' and 'Blow Up' stages which are common in abusive relationships.

Materials: One photocopy of worksheet per participant
Pens/pencils
Optional for GROUP: Flipchart and markers/blackboard and chalk

Activity (Group or Individual):

1. Introduce activity by stating that there is a pattern that is very common in abusive relationships, although it does not apply to all abusive relationships.
2. Refer to the cycle on the page or, in a group, a larger version of the cycle drawn on a flipchart or board. Read or have participant(s) read aloud the descriptions of each stage of the cycle.
3. Ask participant(s) if they can think of examples of this cycle from their own relationships or relationships from a movie, book or TV. If necessary, provide examples of behaviors that might be seen at the various stages such as the following:
   * Honeymoon Stage (Beginning of the relationship): Compliments, buying presents, writing love letters, going out on romantic dates.
   * Tension Building Stage: Accusing the person of flirting with other people, telling the person they're acting stupid, starting arguments about being late. Later in the relationship (after the cycle has escalated) this may include minor battering like pushing, grabbing or shoving.
   * Blow Up Stage: Early in the relationship this might be a minor battering incident like pushing, grabbing or shoving, or verbal abuse and threats. As the cycle repeats the degree of violence may escalate to punching, kicking, breaking bones, shooting, stabbing, etc.
   * Honeymoon Stage (after blow up): Apologizing, making excuses, buying presents, promising to change, making commitments to the relationship, saying s/he couldn't live without the other person.
4. Instruct participant(s) to write the examples they have generated in the spaces provided at the bottom of the page.

Use In Conjunction With:
SEALS+PLUS, *"Serenity,"* (page 23)
SEALS II, *"Repeating Questions,"* (page 67)
SEALS III, *"Coping Tree,"* (page 1)

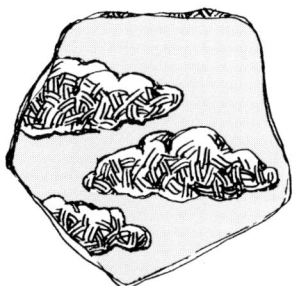

21 Warning Signs
...of an Abusive Person

Following are some common signs that a person is or may turn out to be abusive to his or her intimate partner. Answering yes to one or two questions below does not necessarily mean a person is abusive. However, if any of the questions below are true about you or your partner, you should be cautious about proceeding with the relationship and be sure to address those issues right away, preferably with the help of a counselor.

AM I / IS MY PARTNER A PERSON WHO...   **TRUE of ME**   **TRUE of MY PARTNER**

1. * Was or is abused by a parent? ☐ ☐
2. * Grew up in a home where an adult was abused by another adult? ☐ ☐
3. Gets very serious with boyfriends/girlfriends very quickly - saying "I love you" very early in the relationship, wanting to move in together or get engaged after only a few months, or pressuring partner for a serious commitment? ☐ ☐
4. Comes on very strong, is extremely charming and an overly smooth talker? ☐ ☐
5. Is extremely jealous? ☐ ☐
6. Isolates partner from support systems - wants partner all to themselves, and tries to keep partner from friends, family or outside activities? ☐ ☐
7. Attempts to control what partner wears, what s/he does or who s/he sees? ☐ ☐
8. Is abusive toward other people, especially mother or sisters if he is a male? ☐ ☐
9. Blames others for one's own misbehavior or failures? ☐ ☐
10. Abuses drugs or alcohol? ☐ ☐
11. Has unrealistic expectations, like expecting partner to meet all of one's needs and be the perfect partner? ☐ ☐
12. Is overly sensitive - acts 'hurt' when not getting one's way, takes offense when others disagree with an opinion, gets very upset at small inconveniences that are just a normal part of life? ☐ ☐
13. Has ever been been cruel to animals? ☐ ☐
14. Has ever abused children? ☐ ☐
15. Has ever hit a boyfriend or girlfriend in the past? ☐ ☐
16. Has ever threatened violence, even if it wasn't a 'serious' threat? ☐ ☐
17. Calls partner names, puts him/her down or curses at him/her? ☐ ☐
18. Is extremely moody, and switches quickly from being very nice to exploding in anger? ☐ ☐
19. If a male, believes women are inferior to men and should obey them? ☐ ☐
20. Is intimidating, for example using threatening body language, punching walls or breaking objects? ☐ ☐
21. Holds partner against his/her will to keep him/her from walking away or leaving the room? ☐ ☐

* Numbers 1 and 2 do not indicate a person will be abusive. The majority of children who grow up in abusive homes choose not to be abusive as adults. However, these children have a higher likelihood than other children of growing up to be involved in abusive relationships. These factors should be considered with other factors.

Facilitator's Information for
21 Warning Signs for an Abusive Person

Purpose: To recognize the early warning signs of a potentially abusive personality.

Materials: One photocopy of worksheet per participant
Pens/pencils

Activity (Group or Individual):

1. Introduce activity by reminding participants that abusers do not wear signs across their foreheads saying "I'm Violent." In fact, most abusers are very sweet and charming in the beginning of the relationship and to the rest of the world. However, there are some warning signs that can help you to predict when a person is likely to be abusive. The more of these characteristics a person has, the more likely it is that they are or will turn out to be abusive.
2. Read or have participant(s) read aloud each of the warning signs, and ask for examples of similar behaviors participant(s) have seen in their lives or in the lives of others, on TV or in movies.
3. Instruct participant(s) to check "yes" or "no" to whether the questions are true about themselves and their partners. If they are not currently in a relationship, they can base their answers to the right-hand column on a former relationship or leave it blank.
4. If working with a group, invite participants to share some of their responses or reactions to this activity with the group if they feel comfortable.
5. Process with the following questions:
   * Why do you think (a particular question) might be a sign of abusiveness?
   * If your partner shows this characteristic, how might you address it with him or her?
   * If you have this characteristic, where might you have learned it? How do you feel about it? What can you do if you want to change it?
   * Numbers 8 and 19 address male attitudes and behaviors toward women, but not the other way around. Why is this? (Because gender roles and sexism are one of the major justifications for abusive behavior, which explains why the majority of abuse cases involve a male abusing a female.)

Use In Conjunction With:
SEALS+PLUS, *"Gopher It,"* (page 46)
SEALS II, *"Inner Voice,"* (page 79)
SEALS III, *"Everything in Moderation,"* (page 57)

Why People Stay In Abusive Relationships

Many people recognize they are being mistreated or even abused, but choose to stay in the relationship for a number of reasons. When friends or family members ask them "Why do you stay...?" they may have a hard time explaining. After all, it is never easy to end a relationship, even a hurtful one. Below are some of the common reasons people stay in unhappy or abusive relationships. It you are being mistreated, it might be helpful to look over this list and circle the reasons that might have something to do with your decision to stay.

1. **Love.** You love your partner, and there are still times when your partner is very loving.
2. **Hope.** You have many memories of happy times, and hope those times will return. Your partner may promise to change, or you may think if you do things differently, the abuse will stop.
3. **Making light of the abuse.** Your partner may deny that his or her behavior is abusive, or act like it's not such a big deal, and you want to believe this. It's very painful to admit that someone you love would hurt you, so you might try to convince yourself it's not really that bad.
4. **Blaming yourself.** Your partner might blame you for his or her abusive behavior - saying you made him or her angry, or that you did something to deserve it. A part of you may believe this.
5. **Link between love and violence.** If you grew up in a home where there was violence, or if you were ever hit by a parent and told they were doing it because they love you, you might have learned to think that love and violence go together.
6. **Hopelessness.** You may feel like you'll never be able to be happy, you'll never find a partner who treats you any better, or that all relationships include abuse.
7. **Gender roles.** If you are a woman in a relationship with a man, you may have learned from family, religion or culture that men are supposed to be in charge, can't help being violent, or have the right to discipline their women. You may believe that women have to put up with this behavior and try to keep their men happy.
8. **Embarrassment and shame.** You may not want to admit what's going on to others because you're afraid of what they will think about you.
9. **Financial dependence.** You may depend on your partner for financial support.
10. **Lack of supportive relationships.** You may have become isolated from your friends and family. Or, family and friends may pressure you to stay with your partner.
11. **Fear.** Your partner may have threatened to hurt or kill you or someone you care about if you leave.
12. **Not wanting to be alone.** You may panic at the thought of being without your partner.
13. **Loyalty.** You may feel the right thing to do is to stick with your partner no matter what.
14. **Rescue complex.** You think you can change, fix, or heal your partner if you stay.
15. **Guilt.** Your partner may make you feel guilty about how much it would hurt him or her if you left. S/he may even threaten to commit suicide.
16. **Children.** If you have a child with your partner, you may believe it is best for the child to have two parents who are together.
17. **Dependency on drugs or alcohol.** Many people use drugs or alcohol as a way of coping with abuse, which then makes them less clear and strong and makes it more difficult to leave.
18. Other _____
19. Other _____

(continued on next page)

Why People Stay In Abusive Relationships
(continued)

Whatever your reasons for staying in an abusive relationship, those reasons are very real and very important to you. However it is also important to look at both sides of the situation. Some of your reasons may be based on misunderstandings or myths, and some might be based on fear. If you are struggling with wanting to end the relationship but you can't get past one or more of your reasons for staying, it might help to consider the following statements that give 'the other side' of the argument about each of these reasons.

1. **Love.** No one can argue with the way you feel - your love is real and you can't ignore it. But loving someone doesn't always mean they are healthy for you. Ending your relationship does not mean you will automatically stop loving your partner, but with time your feelings will be less intense as you are able to look at the whole picture. It might help to focus on nurturing your love for yourself and your family or friends. It may seem impossible now, but if you end your relationship, you will someday find another boyfriend or girlfriend to love - and hopefully it will be a healthier love.

2. **Hope.** You are not the cause of the abuse, so nothing you do or change about your behavior will end the abuse. While abusers will usually promise to change during the honeymoon stage, it is rare for an abuser to change while still in a relationship - usually, the only way to stop the abuse is to end the relationship.

3. **Making light of the abuse.** Abuse <u>is</u> a big deal. No one deserves to be abused, and physical abuse is a serious crime that can result in jail time for the abuser.

4. **Blaming yourself.** The fact is there is nothing you can do to make another person hurt you, and no one deserves to be hurt under any circumstances. Everyone is 100% responsible for their own behavior.

5. **Link between love and violence.** Physical abuse is not about love - it's about gaining power and control. Even if violence was normal in your upbringing, the fact is that it is NOT a normal part of a healthy, loving relationship.

6. **Hopelessness.** The idea of being happy without your current partner may seem impossible now, but remember that you are a person who deserves to be treated with respect. There are many people out there who don't abuse!

7. **Gender roles.** A healthy relationship is a partnership based on equality, regardless of gender. If you checked this as a reason for staying, work with a counselor on understanding gender roles.

8. **Embarrassment and shame.** It is true that some people judge or blame people who are being abused because they are not educated about relationship abuse. You must remember that you are not the one doing something wrong, and you have nothing to be ashamed of! Counselors at domestic violence hotlines and agencies will not judge you, and can help you figure out which friends or family members you can talk to.

9. **Financial dependence.** There are ways to become more financially independent, including programs specifically set up for people who are financially trapped in abusive relationships. Your counselor can help you make a plan for financial independence.

10. **Lack of supportive relationships.** Your friends and family may be more willing than you think to help you if you want to end an abusive relationship - but, you may have to develop new supportive relationships. A good place to start is with a support group where you will meet other people who have been in abusive relationships.

11. **Fear.** If you have been threatened, it is very important to develop a safety plan with your counselor before leaving. See the safety plan section in this workbook, and know there are safe homes, shelters and other programs to help you get away from an abuser.

12. **Not wanting to be alone.** You are a strong person who has endured a great deal and while the idea of being alone is scary, you can live without an abusive relationship. Developing other supportive relationships will be helpful.

13. **Loyalty.** Loyalty must be earned. Someone who is supposed to love you, but abuses you, has betrayed you. No reasonable person should expect you to be loyal to someone who abuses you.

14. **Rescue complex.** No amount of loyalty or understanding will change your partner.

15. **Guilt.** Guilt-trips are a way of manipulating you. Your partner is responsible for his or her own actions; you are only responsible for yourself. You have nothing to feel guilty about if you choose to leave an abusive relationship.

16. **Children.** The fact is, witnessing abuse is extremely psychologically damaging to children. A child is better off living with one non-violent parent than with two parents in an abusive relationship. You can work out a way for your child to see the other parent in a safe setting.

17. **Dependency on drugs and alcohol.** If you use drugs or alcohol as a way of coping with abuse, it's important to get treatment for this problem so you can make healthier decisions about your relationships.

18. Other _____

19. Other _____

Facilitator's Information for
Why People Stay In Abusive Relationships

Purpose: To understand common reasons why many people remain in abusive relationships.
To identify some of participants' own reasons for staying in an abusive relationship.
To hear alternative perspectives on reasons for staying in or ending an abusive relationship.

Materials: One photocopy of worksheet per participant
Pens/pencils
Optional: Flipchart and markers/blackboard and chalk

Activity (Group or Individual):
1. Introduce this activity's purpose according to the situation(s) of the group or individual you are working with, as discussed in the facilitator's note.
2. Hand out first page of worksheet and read or have participant(s) read aloud the introductory paragraph.
3. If desired, have the headings of each 'reason' written on flipchart or board for visual aid.
4. Read each item aloud, or have participant(s) take turns reading. Instruct participant(s) to circle the number of each item that has contributed to their staying in an abusive relationship. (If you are working with participant(s) who have not been in abusive relationships, you may want to identify a character from a video you have viewed, a story you have read, or someone the participant knows in real life who is or has been in an abusive relationship. You might develop a short story or skit about an abusive relationship. Ask the participant to guess which factors contributed to that person staying in the relationship.)
5. Discuss and process each item on the list as you go along. Be sure to validate the feelings of participant(s) who disclose their own reasons for staying in an abusive relationship. Without minimizing these feelings, ask participant(s) if they can think of another side to these arguments.
6. After reviewing the list, ask teens if there are reasons for staying in a relationship that are not listed here, and if so, have them write the reason(s) in the space provided.
7. Process this part of the activity by asking participant(s) what feelings this activity brought up, whether they were surprised at some of the things they circled or realized anything new about their reasons for staying, and whether it helps people who have not been in abusive relationships to better understand people who have. Remind participant(s) that all of the reasons discussed are real, legitimate and valid reasons for staying in a relationship.
8. Tell participant(s) that for all the reasons for staying in an abusive relationship, we are now going to look at the other side of the argument.
9. Hand out second page of worksheet and read or have participant(s) read aloud the introductory paragraph.
10. Read or have participant(s) take turns reading aloud each item. Discuss and process each item as you go along, including whether participant(s) had thought of that point while discussing the reasons in the first page of this activity.
11. Process this part of the activity by asking whether this activity has given them anything new to think about or whether they think it will influence their decisions about whether to continue their relationships.

Facilitator's Note: This activity will be most applicable to teens who are currently in relationships that they have identified as abusive. It can be used with teens who have ended abusive relationships to better understand why they stayed as long as they did. For teens who have not been in abusive relationships, or do not identify their relationships as abusive, it can be framed as an activity to help them understand why others might stay in abusive relationships, so they may be able to help a friend or family member who might need their support.

Use In Conjunction With: SEALS+PLUS, *"Be Your Own Best Friend,"* (page 50)
SEALS II, *"Women & Risk Taking,"* (page 54)
SEALS III, *"Personal Network Profile,"* (page 80)

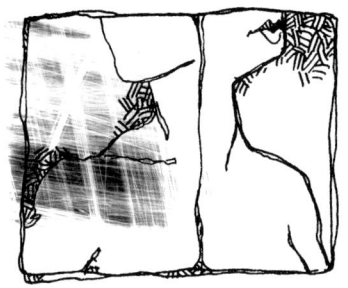

Gender Roles: Men & Women

The term 'gender role' refers to the roles that males and females are expected to play. Often, gender roles are stereotypes. For example, typical gender roles say that men are supposed to be aggressive and not show emotions, while women are supposed to be very emotional and wear dresses and 'feminine' clothes.

In the box below, write as many male gender roles as you can think of. In other words, if someone said, "Act like a man!" what would they mean? Then, think about what happens when a male steps out of the 'Man Box' and doesn't behave that way. Write the names he gets called and the actions that are taken against him that smack him back in the box.

The MAN Box

Words that smack males back in the box

Actions that smack males back in the box

Now do the same exercise for females. What does it mean when someone says, "Act like a lady," and what gets said and done to her when she steps out of the box?

The LADY Box

Words that smack females back in the box

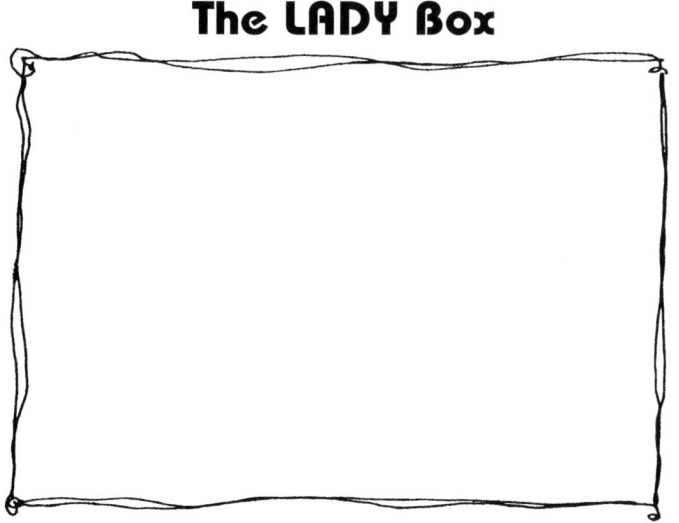

Actions that smack females back in the box

Facilitator's Information for
Gender Roles: Men & Women

Purpose: To understand the meaning of the term 'gender role.'
To identify common gender role expectations.
To understand how people are pressured to conform to gender roles.

Materials: One photocopy of worksheet per participant
Pens/pencils or fine-tipped colored markers
Flipchart and markers/blackboard and chalk

Activity (Group or Individual):
1. Distribute worksheet(s) and read or have participant(s) read the introductory paragraph defining the term gender role.
2. On a flip chart or board write the words 'Act like a man.' Ask participant(s) to imagine that they are a boy of nine or ten, and there is an older man - a father, brother, uncle or coach - who is angry with them and yelling at them to 'Act like a man!' Ask participant(s) what they think is meant by this, and go on to prompt for behaviors that 'Real Men' are supposed to display as they grow into adolescence and adulthood.
3. Write responses under the words 'Act like a man' and instruct participant(s) to write the words in the boxes on their worksheet. If necessary, prompt participant(s) to include examples such as the following: Don't cry, be tough, play with cars and action figures but not with dolls, fight back, don't show emotions, be strong, be in control, pay the bills, play sports, have a lot of sex with women.
4. After completing the list, draw a box around the words. State that we call this 'the Man Box.' Explain that gender roles tell us that all males have to stay in this box at all times, and from the time they are very young they are conditioned to behave in the ways in this box.
5. Ask participant(s) what happens when a male steps out of this box: for example, if a boy plays with dolls, a teenage male cries in front of his friends, or a man chooses to turn down sex with an attractive woman, what happens? What are the words he gets called? (For this exercise, it is best to give participant(s) permission to use their own language including curses or what would normally be considered inappropriate words.)
6. Record answers on one side of the box, and instruct teen(s) to write examples on their worksheet(s) as well. Examples include: 'soft,' 'wimp,' 'mama's boy,' 'wuss,' 'faggot,' etc.
7. Next ask participant(s) what are the things that happen to males who step out of the box. Write answers on the other side of the box and instruct participant(s) to write answers on their worksheet(s). Examples include 'beat up,' 'harassed,' 'isolated,' 'teased,' etc.
8. Conduct the same activity with the "Act like a Lady" box. Examples of lady gender roles are: be emotional, wear dresses, cross your legs, don't be loud, don't fight, don't curse, be polite, be virginal. Examples of words women get called when they step out of the box are: 'tomboy,' 'slut,' 'dyke,' 'bitch,' etc. Examples of actions that smack women back into the box are: they get beat up, fired from their jobs, isolated, blamed for abuse and rape. (Note about abuse and rape: point out that people get abused and raped regardless of whether they are in the box or not, including children, men and elderly people. However when women who step out of the box get abused and raped, they get blamed for it, for example, "What does she expect wearing that slutty dress?")
9. Process this activity by asking participant(s) what it feels like to get called the words and have the things done to you that happen when you step out of the box. Ask if anyone can give an example of having been 'smacked back in the box.' Challenge participant(s) to try to step out of the box in order to be who they are, rather than who the box tells them they should be, and to refrain from smacking other people back in the box.

Use In Conjunction With:
SEALS+PLUS, *"Female Assertive,"* (page 7)
SEALS+PLUS, *"Male Assertive,"* (page 8)
SEALS II, *"A Real Man,"* (page 73)
CROSSING THE BRIDGE, (pages 12, 13)

Gender Roles: Where Do I Stand?

Sometimes our beliefs about males and females are based on messages we've gotten from friends, family, or the media, but haven't really thought too much about. It's important to make our own decisions about what we choose to believe regarding gender roles. Check the boxes below to indicate whether you agree, disagree or are unsure about each statement.

GENDER ROLE STATEMENT	Agree	Disagree	Unsure
Boys are <u>born</u> more violent than girls.			
Girls are <u>born</u> more emotional than boys.			
Women make better parents than men.			
A man should be solely responsible for providing financially for his family.			
A man should have the right to discipline his wife.			
The more often a guy has sex, the more of a man he is.			
The more often a woman has sex, the more of a slut she is.			
The guy should always pay for a date.			
It is okay for someone to hit their girlfriend or boyfriend under some circumstances.			
Both people in a couple should have equal say in all decision-making.			
The music people listen to today contributes to relationship abuse.			
Gay and lesbian people are discriminated against because they do not conform to society's gender roles.			
A man should be embarrassed to be a nurse or secretary because those jobs are for women.			
People should go to jail for beating up their relationship partners.			
Women who dress in overly sexy clothes are asking to get raped or sexually harassed.			
Society generally treats men and women as equals.			
Guys who don't act aggressive will be made fun of by other guys.			
If a girl goes to a guy's room alone with him, then she should expect they're going to have sex.			
A real man could never get raped.			

Facilitator's Information for
Gender Roles: Where Do I Stand?

Purpose: To encourage participants to make informed decisions about their positions on gender issues by provoking discussion and debate on controversial statements about gender roles.

Materials: One photocopy of worksheet per participant
Pens/pencils
Additional for GROUPS: "Agree," "Disagree" and "Unsure" signs
Tape

Activity (Group):
1. Make three signs with the words "Agree," "Disagree" and "Unsure." Tape the signs on three walls around the room.
2. Review the meaning of the term 'gender role' with participants.
3. Instruct participants to stand up, and if necessary push the chairs and tables/desks to the center of the room.
4. Tell group members that you are going to read a statement, and they are to silently decide if they agree with the statement, disagree with the statement or are unsure about the statement. They should then go stand under one of the signs in order to 'vote' on the statement.
5. Once all group members have moved to stand under a sign, allow a limited amount of time for participants from each side to state why they voted as they did. Facilitator should moderate the debate without interjecting his or her opinion - however the facilitator should intervene in victim-blaming if participants do not do so themselves.
6. After debating the issue, ask if anyone would like to change his or her position, and if so, why?
7. Repeat this activity for each of the gender role statements, or as many as time allows.
8. Instruct participants to take their seats. Distribute worksheets.
9. Instruct participants to complete the worksheets based on how they 'vote' for each item.
10. Ask participants if there are other gender role issues that should be included in the debate and if so, to write them in the space provided at the bottom of the page.
11. Process by asking if this activity got anyone to think about issues they had not really thought about before, whether they changed their minds about any issues, and how they think gender roles may be hurtful to men and women.

Activity (Individual):
1. Introduce activity with individual by reviewing the meaning of the term 'gender role' and suggesting that it is important to really think about where we stand on certain gender roles that are common in society.
2. Give teen worksheet and read or have him/her read the introductory paragraph.
3. Read or have teen read each statement, and discuss. Since there are not other young people to engage in debate, facilitator should take more of an active role in guiding the discussion and providing alternative view points, but should ultimately allow the participant to make his or her own decision about whether s/he agrees, disagrees or is unsure about the statement.
4. Process with discussion as in #11 above.

Use In Conjunction With:
SEALS II, *"Real Man,"* (page 73)
SEALS II, *"Letting Go of Other's Expectations,"* (page 74)
SEALS II, *"Letting Go of the Need To Control,"* (page 75)
CROSSING THE BRIDGE, (pages 12, 13)

Facilitator's Information for
Gender Roles: Where Do I Stand?

Purpose: To encourage participants to make informed decisions about their positions on gender issues by provoking discussion and debate on controversial statements about gender roles.

Materials: One photocopy of worksheet per participant
Pens/pencils
Additional for GROUPS: "Agree," "Disagree" and "Unsure" signs
Tape

Activity (Group):
1. Make three signs with the words "Agree," "Disagree" and "Unsure." Tape the signs on three walls around the room.
2. Review the meaning of the term 'gender role' with participants.
3. Instruct participants to stand up, and if necessary push the chairs and tables/desks to the center of the room.
4. Tell group members that you are going to read a statement, and they are to silently decide if they agree with the statement, disagree with the statement or are unsure about the statement. They should then go stand under one of the signs in order to 'vote' on the statement.
5. Once all group members have moved to stand under a sign, allow a limited amount of time for participants from each side to state why they voted as they did. Facilitator should moderate the debate without interjecting his or her opinion - however the facilitator should intervene in victim-blaming if participants do not do so themselves.
6. After debating the issue, ask if anyone would like to change his or her position, and if so, why?
7. Repeat this activity for each of the gender role statements, or as many as time allows.
8. Instruct participants to take their seats. Distribute worksheets.
9. Instruct participants to complete the worksheets based on how they 'vote' for each item.
10. Ask participants if there are other gender role issues that should be included in the debate and if so, to write them in the space provided at the bottom of the page.
11. Process by asking if this activity got anyone to think about issues they had not really thought about before, whether they changed their minds about any issues, and how they think gender roles may be hurtful to men and women.

Activity (Individual):
1. Introduce activity with individual by reviewing the meaning of the term 'gender role' and suggesting that it is important to really think about where we stand on certain gender roles that are common in society.
2. Give teen worksheet and read or have him/her read the introductory paragraph.
3. Read or have teen read each statement, and discuss. Since there are not other young people to engage in debate, facilitator should take more of an active role in guiding the discussion and providing alternative view points, but should ultimately allow the participant to make his or her own decision about whether s/he agrees, disagrees or is unsure about the statement.
4. Process with discussion as in #11 above.

Use In Conjunction With:
SEALS II, *"Real Man,"* (page 73)
SEALS II, *"Letting Go of Other's Expectations,"* (page 74)
SEALS II, *"Letting Go of the Need To Control,"* (page 75)
CROSSING THE BRIDGE, (pages 12, 13)

The Gender Roles Around Us

One of the reasons sexism is so common in our society is that from the time we are very young, we are constantly seeing and hearing stereotypes about the gender roles of men and women. Gender role stereotypes are so much a part of the world we live in, that often we don't even notice they are there. But even when we don't notice them, the messages we get about gender roles have a strong influence on our attitudes, beliefs and behaviors. If we can become more aware of the gender role messages around us, we can make more conscious decisions about which ones to accept and which ones to reject.

Listed below are many different aspects of culture and society. Write examples of gender role stereotypes you have seen in each of these areas.

1. Heroes & Heroines *ex. Male heroes are always rescuing female heroines.*
2. Dance _____
3. Music _____
4. Television _____
5. Movies _____
6. News Media _____
7. Advertisements _____
8. Magazines _____
9. Traditions _____
10. Language _____
11. Values _____
12. Trends _____
13. The Workplace _____
14. School _____
15. Health Care _____
16. Religion _____
17. Economics (money) _____
18. Government _____
19. Social Services _____
20. Family _____
21. Law Enforcement _____

Facilitator's Information for
The Gender Roles Around Us

Purpose: To identify examples of gender roles in different aspects of culture, institutions and interpersonal relationships.

Materials: One photocopy of worksheet per participant
Pens/pencils
Old issues of a variety of different kinds of magazines, newspapers, and TV guides
8 ½" x 11" construction or other heavy paper
Plastic page protectors for 3-ring binders
Glue
Tape
Scissors

Activity (Group or Individual):
1. Distribute worksheet(s) and pen(s) or pencil(s). Place other supplies in reach of all participants.
2. Read or have participant read aloud introductory paragraph. Review the terms listed. Some of the terms may require explanation, discussion and examples: i.e., "economy" may refer to the way a husband and wife handle their family finances, or the way that wealth is distributed in the national economy.
3. While discussing terms and eliciting examples of gender roles in the areas listed, instruct teen(s) to write in examples in the space provided on the worksheet. (For example, heroes always rescuing heroines, doctors are men and nurses are women, men always have to pay for dates.)
4. Tell participant(s) that his/her task is to make a collage that depicts examples of gender role stereotypes in as many of the different areas of culture, institutions and relationships listed as they can. Collages can include pictures or words. As they work on the collages and come up with new examples of gender roles, participant(s) should write the examples on the worksheets.
5. If working with a group, ask for volunteers to present their finished collages to the group, explaining how each picture depicts an example of gender role stereotypes in a particular area of society.
6. If working with portfolios, instruct participant(s) to put collages into the plastic page protectors so they can be placed in their portfolios along with the worksheet.
7. Process activity by reviewing each stereotype and asking participant(s) for an example of a situation where each stereotype does not apply, i.e., "Xena is a strong female heroine on television.", "My doctor is a female."

Follow-up Activity: Make collages that counter gender role stereotypes by depicting men and women in non-stereotypical roles.

Use In Conjunction With:
SEALS+PLUS, *"Black/White,"* (page 22)
SEALS II, *"Breaking Down Our Walls,"* (page 41)
SEALS II, *"Me, My Self Awareness and I,"* (page 51)
CROSSING THE BRIDGE, (pages 12, 13)

My Relationship Role Models
(Where I Got My Relationship Values)

The purpose of this activity is to look carefully at what you learned about relationships from the important people in your life.

Most relationships have positive and negative aspects, but it can be difficult to think about the negative. However this is important, because many times we learn from our role models without even being aware of what we are learning. Then, we often behave in the same way our role models did, and wonder why things aren't turning out any better for us. If you can become aware of what you have learned from your relationship role models, you can then make decisions about what lessons you want to live by, and which ones you want to live without.

Below, please identify a relationship between two people you were around a lot when you were growing up. (You should not be one of the people.)

An intimate relationship I observed while growing up was/is between these two people:
_____ and _____
When I think about their relationship, the first words I think of are: _____
_____, _____, _____
This relationship gave me the impression that men are: _____
This relationship gave me the impression that women are: _____
The best thing I saw about this relationship was/is: _____
_____
The worst thing I saw about this relationship was/is: _____
_____
Most of the time, being around this relationship made/makes me feel: _____
_____
These are some of the ways this relationship has affected me individually: _____
_____
These are some of the ways this relationship has affected my own relationships: _____
_____

Another relationship which I think has affected me was/is between:
_____ and _____
When I think about their relationship, the first words I think of are: _____
_____, _____, _____
This relationship gave me the impression that men are: _____
This relationship gave me the impression that women are: _____
The best thing I saw about this relationship was/is: _____
_____
The worst thing I saw about this relationship was/is: _____
_____
Most of the time, being around this relationship made/makes me feel: _____
_____
These are some of the ways this relationship has affected me individually: _____
_____
These are some of the ways this relationship has affected my own relationships: _____
_____

My Relationship Role Models
(Where I Got My Relationship Values) (continued)

Another relationship which I think has affected me was/is between:
_____ and _____
When I think about their relationship, the first words I think of are: _____
_____, _____, _____
This relationship gave me the impression that men are: _____
This relationship gave me the impression that women are: _____
The best thing I saw about this relationship was/is: _____
_____
The worst thing I saw about this relationship was/is: _____
_____
Most of the time, being around this relationship made/makes me feel: _____
_____
These are some of the ways this relationship has affected me individually: _____
_____
These are some of the ways this relationship has affected my own relationships: _____
_____

Another relationship which I think has affected me was/is between:
_____ and _____
When I think about their relationship, the first words I think of are: _____
_____, _____, _____
This relationship gave me the impression that men are: _____
This relationship gave me the impression that women are: _____
The best thing I saw about this relationship was/is: _____
_____
The worst thing I saw about this relationship was/is: _____
_____
Most of the time, being around this relationship made/makes me feel: _____
_____
These are some of the ways this relationship has affected me individually: _____
_____
These are some of the ways this relationship has affected my own relationships: _____
_____

Facilitator's Information for
My Relationship Role Models (Where I got My Relationship Values)

Purpose: To understand how the relationships of parents, caregivers and other role models have influenced the participants' relationship patterns.

Materials: One photocopy of each worksheet per participant
Pens/pencils
Optional: List of 'feeling' words or EMOTIONS© page from SEALS+PLUS.
Optional: 'Sample' page completed in advance, with examples from a fictional relationship.

Activity (Group or Individual):
1. Introduce the activity with a discussion about the importance of understanding how we have been influenced by the relationships we saw growing up. Discuss the term 'role model,' and clarify that while we often use the term to refer only to positive role models, our role models can set both positive and negative examples.
2. Distribute worksheet(s) and read or have a participant read the introductory paragraph. Emphasize the idea that this activity may bring up difficult emotions, especially for people who have experienced abuse in the home. Tell teen(s) that if they choose to acknowledge negative aspects of a person's relationship, this does not mean that they are putting that person down or ignoring the positive aspects of that person or that relationship. Remind them that most parents or loved ones would want the participant(s) to learn from their own experiences, both negative and positive. Clarify that the participant should not be one of the people identified. This activity is about relationships that we observed, not relationships between others and ourselves.
3. Instruct teen(s) to identify the relationship that they think had the greatest affect on them, and write the names of the people in the first box. This could simply be the relationship they were around the most, often parents or caretakers, although sometimes a relationship between people who they didn't live with could have made an extremely negative or extremely positive impression.
4. Read or have participant(s) read each subsequent statement, and instruct them to fill in their responses in the space provided. It may be necessary to get teen(s) started by providing examples of feeling words, and/or offer a 'sample' page filled out based on fictional relationships.
5. After completing the first box, instruct participant(s) to choose two or three other relationships that affected them and complete the boxes on this page and on the second worksheet.

Follow-up Activity: Choosing My Relationship Values, (page 59)

Facilitator's Note: This activity can bring up a lot of difficult emotions and can be clinically sensitive. It should only be undertaken with a group that is well into the intimacy stages of group development, or in individual sessions.

Use In Conjunction With:
SEALS+PLUS, *"Influential People,"* (page 51)
SEALS II, *"Envisioning Female Role Models,"* (page 49)
SEALS II, *"Envisioning Male Role Models,"* (page 50)
CROSSING THE BRIDGE, (pages 49, 51)

Facilitator's Information for
My Relationship Role Models (Where I got My Relationship Values)

Purpose: To understand how the relationships of parents, caregivers and other role models have influenced the participants' relationship patterns.

Materials: One photocopy of each worksheet per participant
Pens/pencils
Optional: List of 'feeling' words or EMOTIONS© page from SEALS+PLUS.
Optional: 'Sample' page completed in advance, with examples from a fictional relationship.

Activity (Group or Individual):
1. Introduce the activity with a discussion about the importance of understanding how we have been influenced by the relationships we saw growing up. Discuss the term 'role model,' and clarify that while we often use the term to refer only to positive role models, our role models can set both positive and negative examples.
2. Distribute worksheet(s) and read or have a participant read the introductory paragraph. Emphasize the idea that this activity may bring up difficult emotions, especially for people who have experienced abuse in the home. Tell teen(s) that if they choose to acknowledge negative aspects of a person's relationship, this does not mean that they are putting that person down or ignoring the positive aspects of that person or that relationship. Remind them that most parents or loved ones would want the participant(s) to learn from their own experiences, both negative and positive. Clarify that the participant should not be one of the people identified. This activity is about relationships that we observed, not relationships between others and ourselves.
3. Instruct teen(s) to identify the relationship that they think had the greatest affect on them, and write the names of the people in the first box. This could simply be the relationship they were around the most, often parents or caretakers, although sometimes a relationship between people who they didn't live with could have made an extremely negative or extremely positive impression.
4. Read or have participant(s) read each subsequent statement, and instruct them to fill in their responses in the space provided. It may be necessary to get teen(s) started by providing examples of feeling words, and/or offer a 'sample' page filled out based on fictional relationships.
5. After completing the first box, instruct participant(s) to choose two or three other relationships that affected them and complete the boxes on this page and on the second worksheet.

Follow-up Activity: Choosing My Relationship Values, (page 59)

Facilitator's Note: This activity can bring up a lot of difficult emotions and can be clinically sensitive. It should only be undertaken with a group that is well into the intimacy stages of group development, or in individual sessions.

Use In Conjunction With:
SEALS+PLUS, *"Influential People,"* (page 51)
SEALS II, *"Envisioning Female Role Models,"* (page 49)
SEALS II, *"Envisioning Male Role Models,"* (page 50)
CROSSING THE BRIDGE, (pages 49, 51)

Choosing My Relationship Values

While many people carry on the patterns of behavior they learned from their 'relationship role models,' you don't necessarily have to. You can decide which patterns are healthy for you, and which ones are not. You can choose to continue or change patterns of behavior by making conscious decisions about what you want your relationships to look like. You can choose your 'Relationship Values,' and live according to the values you choose.

1. These are the values I learned from my relationship role models which I believe are healthy for me and I choose to keep as my own values:

_____
_____
_____
_____

2. These are the values I learned from my relationship role models which I believe are unhealthy for me, and I choose to reject:

_____
_____
_____
_____

3. These are relationship values that I have developed on my own, and choose to add to my list of relationship values to live by:

_____
_____
_____
_____

4. These are relationship values that I have seen or experienced, which I do not believe are healthy for me, and I now choose to reject:

_____
_____
_____
_____

Facilitator's Information for
Choosing My Relationship Values

Purpose: To identify learned relationship values.
To make conscious decisions about which values to keep and which ones to reject.

Materials: One photocopy of worksheet per participant
Copies of completed worksheets <u>My Relationship Role Models</u>
Pens/pencils
Additional for GROUPS: Flipchart and markers/blackboard and chalk

Activity (Group or Individual):
1. This activity should be done as a follow-up to <u>My Relationship Role Models</u>. If it is done in a separate session, begin by reviewing that activity.
2. Distribute worksheet(s) and read or have participant(s) read aloud the introductory paragraph.
3. If working with a group, draw two columns on board or flip chart, titled "Values to Keep" and "Values to Reject."
4. Instruct participant(s) to read over <u>My Relationship Role Models</u> and find all of the values they learned that they believe are healthy, and write them in the space provided in number one. If working with a group, invite participant(s) to share with the group the values they choose to keep, and write those values in the column on the flipchart or board.
5. Next instruct participant(s) to find all of the values they learned that they believe are unhealthy, and write them in the space in #2. Again, ask group participants to share their responses and record them on flipchart or board.
6. Continue with numbers three and four, allowing participant(s) to add their own values to keep or reject. To add to the discussion, suggest participant(s) think about relationships in videos, movies, television shows or even values that are promoted in music they listen to.
7. Close this activity by reminding participant(s) that as they gain more experience in life and in relationships, their list of values on both sides will grow; they should feel free to add to the list.
8. Process by asking participant(s) how this activity might help them have healthier relationships, if it would be useful to share these values with their partners and if so, at what point in the relationship would they do this? Would they ask their partners to also share their values? What would happen if they and their partners had opposing values?

Use In Conjunction With:
SEALS+PLUS, *"Influential People,"* (page 51)
SEALS II, *"Envisioning Female Role Models,"* (page 49)
SEALS II, *"Envisioning Male Role Models,"* (page 50)
CROSSING THE BRIDGE, (pages 33, 37, 38, 43, 49, 50)

What's Age Got To Do With It?

**It's only natural to admire older men and women.
So what's the big deal when it comes to going out with someone older?**

The answer depends on a lot of things. In many cultures, it is normal and even expected for girls to date or marry much older men. In most of those cultures, it is the man who is considered the head of the family. In modern Western cultures, where we are moving more toward equality of the sexes, it is most common to date people within one or two years of your own age - at least during the teenage years. In fact, it is illegal in the U.S. for an adult to have sex with a minor - this is called statutory rape.

We're not saying that everyone who dates a younger partner has bad intentions or turns out to be abusive. But sometimes, people date people much younger than them because they think they will be able to manipulate and control a younger person. It makes sense that if someone is seeking a true and equal partnership, they would usually seek a person of a similar age, maturity and experience level.

Below are some of the risks involved in going out with someone much older than you.
Check any that apply to you.

If you go out with an older person, you may...

☐ Grow apart from your friends and stop doing things that are normal for people your age.

☐ Become physically isolated when you're out with your partner, because you're at your partner's place, in his or her car, or going to unfamiliar places. This may put you at greater risk for date rape.

☐ Make a habit of lying to your parents/guardians if you're staying at your partner's place or hiding the relationship from them. You may get into a major conflict with your family over this.

☐ Start or increase drinking alcohol if your partner's over 21 and drinks regularly.

☐ Start or increase using drugs because your partner has easy access and uses drugs a lot.

☐ Be expected to act certain ways or do certain things that you're not ready for, just because you're hanging out with older people.

☐ Begin to feel badly about yourself if your partner gives you the message that you're 'stupid' when you don't know something that most people your age wouldn't know, or you're 'childish and immature' when you act ways that are normal for your age.

☐ Find it harder to say no to sex because you know your older partner is probably used to having sex with dates.

☐ Be at risk for sexually transmitted diseases and AIDS, because an older person who has had more sex partners is more likely to have been exposed.

☐ Begin to feel like your partner acts more like your parent - telling you how to dress, how to act, always correcting you, etc.

☐ Let your grades slip in school, because school is not a focus in your partner's life so it may seem less important to you.

☐ Get pregnant, thinking your partner will take care of you, but you may wind up trying to raise a child alone.

☐ Wind up being controlled emotionally, financially, sexually and/or physically, because an older partner starts out with more power and might take advantage of it.

Facilitator's Information for
What's Age Got To Do With It?

Purpose: To become aware of the risk factors associated with dating much older partners.

Materials: One photocopy of worksheet per participant
Pens/pencils
Optional: Information about your state's statutory rape laws

Activity (Group or Individual):
1. Distribute worksheet(s) and read or have participant(s) read aloud the introductory paragraphs. Discuss and process terms and concepts as necessary.
2. Read or have participant(s) read aloud each item on the list, discussing each item as you go and allowing participant(s) to share relevant experiences when they are comfortable doing so.
3. As you review each item on the list, instruct participant(s) who have dated or are dating much older people to check the items that have happened or are happening to them. Instruct participant(s) who have not dated much older people to check the items that they think would be a problem if they were to date an older person in the future.
4. Process with the following questions:
   * What do you think attracts younger people to older people?
   * What do you think attracts older people to younger people?
   * Do you or anyone you know come from a cultural background that encourages dating between much older and younger people?
   * How are the dynamics the same or different when you are talking about a younger girl and older man, a younger boy and older woman, younger and older males or younger and older females?
   * Do any participants' parents have big age differences? How and why have age differences changed over the years?
   * How does being much older help someone to control their younger partner?
   * In an abusive relationship, how might being involved with a much older abuser be different from being involved with an abuser your own age?

Facilitator's Note: This activity will often prompt students to ask a lot of questions about the details of statutory rape. The statutory rape laws vary from state to state, and you can contact your local district attorney's office's sex crimes division for information. It is usually effective to explain that the purpose of these laws is to protect young people who have less power than much older people, and therefore are not always able to make a healthy decision about whether to consent to sex.

In discussing cultural issues, it is important not to judge or devalue different cultural norms. Remind participants that the purpose of this activity is not to judge what age differences are right or wrong, but to become aware of some of the risk factors for abuse.

Use In Conjunction With:
SEALS+PLUS, *"Decision Making,"* (page 45)
SEALS II, *"The HIV Infection/AIDS Quiz,"* (page 63)
SEALS III, *"Evaluate Your Relationship,"* (page 50)

Violence At Home:
What You Can Do When the Adults at Home are Fighting

1. **Don't get in the middle of a fight.** Children, especially adolescent boys, are often injured while trying to protect a parent who's being abused. This won't help anyone. Instead, get away from the fighting and go to a neighbor's to stay safe and ask for help.

2. **Call the police if you witness violence.** This is the best way to protect a parent who's being abused. It may feel like you are betraying your parents, but if things are this out of control, your family needs help and this may be the only way of getting it.

3. **Call a Domestic Violence Hotline.** (The National Hotline number is 1-800-799-7233.) The counselors can help you figure out how to handle the situation.

4. **Make a 'Safety Plan.'** This is a written plan for what you will do to protect yourself and your family if there is violence at home. You can be better prepared for violence if you practice "what if" scenarios and plan things like all the ways you could get out of the house and get to a phone, and how you could help younger brothers and sisters stay safe. You can also make up a 'code word' to let family, neighbors or friends know that there is danger.

5. **Know that it is never your fault.** The only person who is responsible for abuse is the abuser, no matter what excuses are given. Your parents are responsible for taking care of you, not the other way around.

6. **Try not to blame the person who's being abused.** Again, the abuser may give excuses, but remember that no one deserves to be abused and the person who's being violent is 100% responsible for his/her behavior.

7. **Get help dealing with your emotions.** Violence in the home always has negative emotional effects on kids. Find someone you trust to talk to about what's going on at home - a school counselor, a counselor at a community center, or someone at a domestic violence hotline. (You can call a hotline confidentially.)

8. **Make healthy choices about your own behavior.** Even if you've seen violence at home, you can choose not to be violent yourself. It is never okay for you to hit your brothers or sisters, kids at school, or anyone else. Learn ways to express your feelings without using violence.

9. _____
   _____
   _____

Facilitator's Information for
Violence At Home: What You Can Do When the Adults at Home are Fighting

Purpose: To identify strategies for dealing with violence between adults at home.

Materials: One photocopy of worksheet per participant
Pens/pencils
Flipchart and markers/blackboard and chalk

Activity (Group or Individual):
1. Optionally, begin by showing opening segment of the video The Viscous Cycle of Abuse (listed in resource section.)
2. Prompt teen(s) to brainstorm a list of feelings that might be experienced by a child who witnesses violence between adults at home, and write list on flipchart or board. Include feelings that a child might experience during and immediately after the violence, as well as longer-term emotions.
3. Prompt teen(s) to brainstorm another list of things a young person could do if they are witnessing violence at home, and write list on flipchart or board. Include things they could do at the time of the violence, immediately after, and on an ongoing basis.
4. Distribute worksheet(s) and pens/pencils.
5. Read or have participant(s) read aloud each item on the sheet, and discuss. Instruct participant(s) to check any of the things they have done in the past, and to put a star next to any of the items they decide they will do in the future.
6. Invite teen(s) to share with group members/counselor any strategies they have used in the past and how well they have or have not worked.
7. Discuss the concept of safety planning in more detail. For teen(s) who are currently experiencing violence in the home, work with them to develop at least a verbal safety plan at this time, and follow up with a written safety plan.

Use In Conjunction With:
SEALS+PLUS, *"Look for Alternatives,"* (page 20)
SEALS II, *"Awareness Journal,"* (page 52)
SEALS III, *"Come To Recovery Island,"* (page 47)

The Do's and Don'ts of Starting A Relationship

Many people want to be in a romantic relationship but don't know how to get one started. *If this sounds like you, it's important to first look at your reasons for wanting to be in a relationship. Is it because many of your friends have boyfriends or girlfriends? You're lonely? You want to prove something? Your friends are pressuring you about having sex? These aren't good reasons to start a relationship. You need to recognize that it's okay, even healthy, not to have a boyfriend or girlfriend. There are also many benefits to leaving a friend a friend. But if you find yourself attracted to someone and don't know how to start up a relationship with them, here are some suggestions.*

DO:

- Be confident. This is easier said than done, but you can train yourself to be confident by practicing your assertiveness skills, reminding yourself of all of your strengths, and working on your self-esteem with 'positive self-talk.'
- Notice something about the person you're interested in - something you have in common or something that you can compliment them on to strike up a conversation. But don't fake it - be sincere when you give compliments.
- Ask the person to do something 'non-threatening,' like going to a sports event or a park during the day, or going out with a group of mutual friends.
- If the person agrees to go out, meet and hang out in a public place, and avoid being isolated with a person you don't know that well.
- Show interest in the other person. Ask about their likes and dislikes, family and friends, values and beliefs, goals and dreams.
- Be honest about who you are and what you want out of the relationship. Of course, this requires knowing yourself first!
- Call when you say you will.
- Be very careful about meeting people through the internet. If you're going to meet face-to-face, always do it in a public place with friends around.
- Trust your instincts. If you're uncomfortable with a person or a situation, don't be afraid to do what you need to do to feel safe.
- Bring your own money on a date and be prepared to pay. It's often awkward knowing who should pay, but it shouldn't be assumed that it's the guy's role. Often women want to pay for themselves so they can remain independent and not feel like they 'owe' anything.
- Be aware of the signs of healthy and unhealthy relationships (see activities in this workbook.)
- Accept "No" for an answer. If the person seems unsure about whether to go out with you, take the time try to get to know each other better, and if they seem interested, try again. However, if they have clearly said that they are not interested, respect their decision and move on.
- _____

DON'T:

- Wait for someone you're interested in to come to you. It's okay for guys and girls to make the first move.
- Use teasing or obnoxious 'playing around' to get someone's attention.
- Play 'hard to get' or other mind games.
- Make a judgement about someone based on what group they hang out with, whether they're popular or not, or what your friends would say about them.
- Be aggressive or come on too strong. Don't try to force someone into going out with you if they're not interested.
- Go alone to the other person's home or invite them to your home, get in a car alone with them, or become isolated with someone you don't know very well.
- Spend all night talking about your ex.
- Get drunk or high in order to 'loosen up' and be confident on a date. Chances are you'll wind up regretting it.
- Send mixed messages, especially about sex. Be aware of your body language and other non-verbal communication.
- Pressure anyone into sex, or get them high or drunk to get them to have sex. Remember, date rape includes using verbal coercion like threats or manipulation, drugs and alcohol or physical force to get someone to have sex when they don't want to.
- Do anything you don't want to, including anything sexual, just because you want the other person to like you or don't want to hurt their feelings.
- _____

Facilitator's Information for
The Do's and Don'ts of Starting A Relationship

Purpose: To identify pros and cons of being single versus being in a relationship. To identify safe and healthy strategies for initiating a relationship. To understand dangerous or unhealthy behaviors in starting a relationship.

Materials: One photocopy of worksheet per participant
Pens/pencils
Flipchart and markers/blackboard and chalk

Activity (Group):
1. Ask participants if any of them has ever been single for a time but wanted to be in a relationship. Ask reasons why people want to be in relationships, and write a list of those reasons on the flipchart or board.
2. Ask participants, of the reasons for wanting to be in a relationship that are listed, which ones do they think are healthy reasons and which are not? Put a star next to the healthy reasons and put a line through the unhealthy reasons.
3. Next, prompt participants to brainstorm a list of 'pros' and 'cons' of being single. Write the list on board or flip chart, and discuss as necessary.
4. Conduct one of the following two activities, or both if time allows:
   A) Ask for two volunteers to do a role-play. Set up the role-play as follows: one character has weighed the pros and cons of being single, and decided s/he really wants to be in a relationship. S/he doesn't know the other character, but has seen him/her around school and is interested in getting to know and maybe going out with him/her. Instruct volunteers to role-play the one character approaching the other. After the role-play, allow other teens to give advice to the characters or to replace the characters and do more role-plays.
   B) Split the participants into two or more small groups of 3-4 teens each. Tell each group they are to pretend they are advice columnists for a teen magazine, and they give advice about love and romance. Allow each group to come up with the name of its advice column. They are to write a response to one of the following letters from a reader (make up or have teens make up more letters if necessary):
      * "Dear _____: There's a guy at school I have a total crush on but he doesn't know I exist. I'm kind of shy and don't know how to get him to notice me. What should I do? Signed, Crushed"
      * "Dear _____: All my friends have girlfriends and are giving me a hard time because I'm not 'getting any.' I need to get a girl quick so I can get them off my back, but every time I try to approach a chick I strike out. Help! Signed, Needs Some."
      * "Dear _____: This guy I met at the pizza place where I hang out asked me out and I said yes, mostly because I didn't want to hurt his feelings. I guess he seems nice but I don't know anything about him because he doesn't go to my school. I haven't gone out with anyone in a long time so in a way I wouldn't mind going out with him, but what if I don't like him and then I'm stuck with him all night? What should I do? Signed, Confused."
      * "Dear_____: I finally got up the nerve to ask out this girl I've been wanting to talk to for a while. I said I'd pick her up at her house next weekend, but I have no idea what to do with her after that. Should I just bring her to hang out on the corner with my friends, or what? Signed, Idea-less"
      Have each group share its response with the other groups and discuss.
5. Distribute worksheets and read or have participants read through the introductory paragraph and the Do's & Don'ts, processing as you go along. Allow teens to add to the lists in the spaces provided.

Activity (Individual):
1. Begin activity by facilitating a discussion about the pros and cons of being single vs. in a relationship, and why participant does or does not want to be in a relationship at this time.
2. Give teen worksheet and read or have him/her read aloud the introductory paragraph and the do's and don'ts, processing together as you go along.
3. If teen is interested in learning how to initiate a relationship, suggest a role-play as in #4 above, with the participant playing him or her self and the counselor playing the role of the person s/he is asking out. Or, read some of the letters asking for advice, and ask participant what kind of advice s/he would give, and process.

Use In Conjunction With:
SEALS+PLUS, *"Your Body Can Speak,"* (page 17)
SEALS II, *"Good Manners,"* (page 65)
SEALS II, *"Social Skills 4 Life,"* (page 66)
CROSSING THE BRIDGE, (pages 49, 50, 51)

What to Look for in a Partner

What makes a relationship healthy? Two people who value equality and respect make a good start. Here are some characteristics you may want to consider in a potential boyfriend or girlfriend.

- ☐ Someone who supports your relationships with friends and family members. S/he is willing to spend time with your friends and family to get to know them, and at the same time gives you space to spend time alone with them.
- ☐ Someone who maintains his or her own friendships, and wants you to get to know his or her friends.
- ☐ Someone who supports your personal growth. S/he encourages you to participate in activities that are good for you, like team sports or other athletic activities, clubs or groups you belong to, a job or a hobby.
- ☐ Someone who continues his or her own interests in outside activities, such as sports, clubs or groups, a job or a hobby.
- ☐ Someone who asks your opinion.
- ☐ Someone who is comfortable with your having different opinions from him or her, and does not take it as a personal insult when you disagree.
- ☐ Someone who you feel comfortable expressing your feelings and emotions with.
- ☐ Someone who talks and listens.
- ☐ Someone who accepts responsibility for his or her own behavior, feelings and thoughts.
- ☐ Someone who can apologize when he or she is wrong, and accept your apology when you're wrong.
- ☐ Someone who considers the relationship a partnership.
- ☐ Someone who shares in decision-making.
- ☐ Someone who expects both partners to control their own money, and never uses money as a way of getting what s/he wants.
- ☐ Someone who treats other people with respect. (If a male, one who treats his mother and sisters with respect.)
- ☐ Someone who is secure enough not to feel threatened by your friendships with people of either sex.
- ☐ Someone who trusts you and expects to be trusted.
- ☐ Someone who encourages you in your goals and dreams.
- ☐ Someone who makes positive statements about your strengths.
- ☐ Someone who you feel safe with.
- ☐ Someone who can resolve conflicts without resorting to violence or put-downs.
- ☐ _____
- ☐ _____

Facilitator's Information for
What to Look for in a Partner

Purpose: To identify some characteristics of a potentially healthy relationship partner.

Materials: One photocopy of worksheet per participant
Pens/pencils

Activity (Group or: Individual):
1. Introduce activity by reading or having a participant read aloud the opening paragraph.
2. Engage participant(s) in discussion about why it might be important to think about the signs of a healthy partner before you get involved in a new relationship.
3. Read or have participant(s) read aloud each item in the list, and discuss as appropriate, encouraging participant(s) to give examples of these behaviors from their own relationships or relationships they are familiar with. Facilitator may want to process each item by asking "How would you know a person is 'someone who...'; what specific behaviors would you see or not see?"
4. Instruct participant(s) to decide which items are important to them, and check the ones that they will consider next time they begin a relationship. Or, participants who are considering beginning a new relationship or currently in a relationship may check the items that apply to their partner or potential partner.
5. After completing the activity, offer participant(s) blank copies of the worksheet to keep for future use, when they are considering a new relationship.

Use In Conjunction With:
SEALS+PLUS, *"Let's Pretend a Friend,"* (page 71)
SEALS II, *"Savvy Socializing,"* (page 37)
SEALS III, *"Creative Love, Creating Love,"* (page 49)

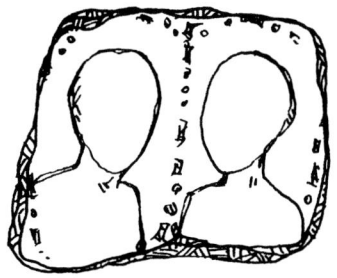

Understanding Boundaries

One important way to take care of yourself is to set strong and healthy boundaries around yourself and your life. A Boundary is like an invisible line around you. It is what separates you from other people. It is the line between what you are comfortable with and what you are uncomfortable with, what is acceptable to you and what is unacceptable to you. Boundaries help protect not only our physical safety, but also our emotional well-being.

Healthy boundaries are flexible. For example, you might open up your boundaries to let people you trust closer to you - you might share more information with them and feel more comfortable being physically close to them. But with people you don't know as well or people you distrust, you will probably keep your boundaries closed more tightly by not getting too personal.

<u>DIFFERENT BOUNDARIES WITH DIFFERENT RELATIONSHIPS</u>

In **circle 1** around "you", write the names of the people who are closest to you, and who you open up your boundaries the most for. In **circle 2**, write the names of a few people who you have good relationships with but are not as close as the people in the inner circle. In **circle 3**, mention names of people who you have relationships with that are not very personal. Is there anyone who has given you good reason not to trust them - who you feel you have to protect yourself from? Write these names on the **outside of the solid line**, which indicates that your boundaries are very firm with them.

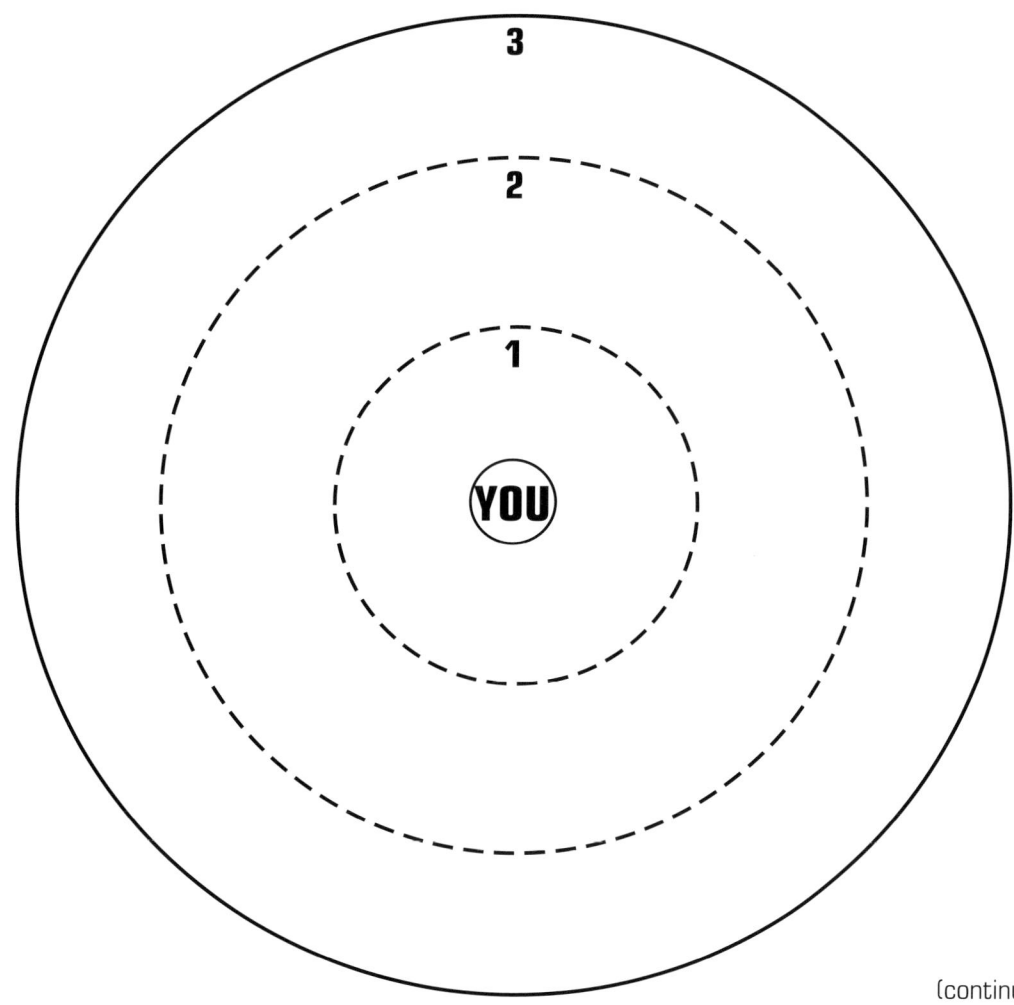

(continued on next page)

Understanding Boundaries
(continued)

Boundaries aren't just for controlling which people we want to be close to us. Healthy boundaries allow us to control all sorts of things in our lives, including our own behavior and which behaviors we will accept from others. For example, a person may be comfortable with kissing her partner in public, but 'draw the line' at her partner touching her in a sexual way in front of other people. That 'line' is her boundary. Abuse happens when one person violates another person's boundaries.

Think about your boundaries around physical touch, sexual behavior, language, morals and values. Write some examples of your boundaries below.

BEHAVIORS I'M COMFORTABLE WITH	"Boundary"	**BEHAVIORS I'M UNCOMFORTABLE WITH**
_____		_____
_____		_____
_____		_____
_____		_____
_____		_____
_____		_____
_____		_____
_____		_____
_____		_____
_____		_____
_____		_____
_____		_____
_____		_____
_____		_____

Facilitator's Information for
Understanding Boundaries

Purpose: To understand the concept of boundaries and define participants' own personal boundaries.

Materials: One photocopy of each worksheet per participant
Pens/pencils
Optional: Flipchart and markers/blackboard and chalk

Activity (Group:)
1. Begin the group with the following 'icebreaker': Instruct group members to form two lines facing each other, standing about ten feet apart. Participants should slowly walk towards their partner, and get as close as they feel comfortable. At the point that they do not feel comfortable getting any physically closer, participants should put their hand up and say "stop!" Process with a brief discussion of the concept of personal space, and explain to participants that in doing this activity they have set boundaries around their personal space.
2. Distribute copies of the first page of Understanding Boundaries and read or have participants read aloud the introductory paragraphs and discuss, clarifying concepts as necessary.
3. Read or have participant read aloud directions under 'Different Boundaries with Different Relationships.'
4. Draw a copy of the diagram on flip chart or board and complete an example by putting 'parents,' 'best friends,' 'sister' and 'boyfriend/girlfriend' in the circle 1; 'other friends' in the circle 2; 'teachers' and 'neighbors' in the circle 3 and "someone who hurt me" outside of the solid circle.
5. Instruct participants to fill in the names of people they have different relationships and different boundaries with in the appropriate circles.
6. After participants have completed the diagram, invite them to share with the group what names they wrote and why.
7. Distribute copies of the second page of Understanding Boundaries and read or have a participant read aloud the introductory paragraph and discuss, clarifying concepts as necessary.
8. Write 'Comfortable' and 'Uncomfortable' on board or flip chart and draw a line between the two. Ask participants to offer examples of behaviors that might be acceptable or unacceptable to different people.
9. Instruct participants to fill in behaviors they are comfortable/uncomfortable with on either side of the 'Boundary' line on the worksheet.
10. Process this activity with the following questions:
    * What are some boundaries you have drawn in your relationships?
    * How do you make sure other people are aware of your boundaries?
    * Have you ever seen boundaries that are too inflexible, so that people don't allow anyone close to them or have trouble trusting anyone at all? Why do you think people might develop such rigid boundaries?
    * What are some of the reasons people sometimes have difficulty setting strong boundaries?
    * How could it be helpful in your relationships for you to be clear about your own boundaries?
    * Do you think it would be helpful to practice setting boundaries?

Activity (Individual:)
1. Give participant copies of both worksheets and read or have teen read aloud the introductory paragraph and directions on the first worksheet, discussing and clarifying concepts as necessary.
2. Work with teen to fill in the names of people with whom they have different boundaries in the appropriate circles. If necessary, prompt with examples as in #4 above.
3. On second worksheet, read or have participant read aloud the introductory paragraph and directions, discussing and clarifying concepts as necessary.
4. Assist participant in brainstorming behaviors he or she is comfortable and uncomfortable with, and writing those behaviors in the space provided.
5. Process as in #10 above.

Follow-up Activity: Practicing Boundary Setting, (page 72)

Use In Conjunction With:
SEALS+PLUS, 'No-One Is an Island,' (page 63)
SEALS II, 'Developing Boundaries,' (page 39)
SEALS III, 'Understanding Personal Boundaries,' (page 55)
CROSSING THE BRIDGE, (pages 30, 49)

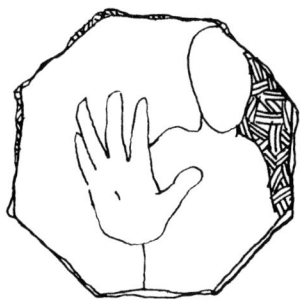

Practicing Boundary Setting

Because you are in charge of your life, you are the only person who should be able to control your boundaries. Abuse happens when one person violates another person's boundaries. That's why it's important to be very clear for yourself, and very clear to others, what your boundaries are. If you have weak or uncertain boundaries, others are more likely to abuse you; if you have strong and clear boundaries, you will be more likely to remain in control of your life and keep yourself safe emotionally and physically.

Decide whether each situation below is an example of setting strong boundaries, or is an example of weak boundaries. Write WEAK or STRONG on the line.

Joseph and Manuel are playing around and Manuel smacks Joseph on the back of the head. Respectfully, but without smiling or laughing, Joseph makes eye contact with Manuel and says "Listen Manuel, I know you're only playing but I don't like people putting their hands on me. Don't smack me like that again." _____

Sandra and Sam are kissing. Sam starts to push up Sandra's shirt but Sandra doesn't want to go any further. She quietly says "Umm, I don't know if we should be doing this, Sam." Sam says "It's okay, don't worry..." and continues. Sandra lets him even though it makes her uncomfortable, then finally says "It's getting late – I really have to go home." _____

Naomi and Sherika are shopping when Naomi tells Sherika she's going to slip a pair of earrings into her bag. Sherika says, "I'm not into shoplifting. Please don't do that when I'm around. If I knew you were planning on shoplifting, I wouldn't have come shopping with you." _____

Now you practice setting boundaries... Help the characters set boundaries by writing on the line what they should do or say to set strong boundaries.

Jessie forgot his homework at Michael's house and snaps "Why didn't you remind me to get my homework – now I'm going to fail!" (What can Michael say to set boundaries in terms of what he will take responsibility for?)
_____

Rich has been friendly with Jason for a while, and thinks he's a nice guy. When his friend Paul gets into an argument with Jason and starts talking bad about him, Paul expects Rich to be against Jason too.
(What can Rich say to set boundaries in terms of his friendships?)
_____

Eric lent Jeff $10 months ago and Jeff never paid him back. Now Jeff is asking him to borrow money again.
(What can Eric say to set boundaries in terms of lending and borrowing money?)
_____

Taria needed help with college applications, so she made an appointment to see her guidance counselor Ms. Ruiz during 6th period. Taria shows up at the beginning of 7th period, but it is Ms. Ruiz' lunch period and Ms. Ruiz finds it very important to take her break every day to reduce her stress. (What can Ms. Ruiz say to set boundaries in terms of her time?)
_____

What is a boundary you need to set in a relationship?

Person I need to set a boundary with: _____

Boundary I need to set: _____

What I can say or do to set this boundary: _____

Facilitator's Information for
Practicing Boundary Setting

Purpose: To differentiate between weak and strong boundaries.
To practice boundary setting.

Materials: One photocopy of worksheet per participant
Pens/pencils
Optional: Flipchart and markers/blackboard and chalk

Activity (Group):
1. This activity should be done as a follow-up to Understanding Boundaries. Begin by reviewing that activity and relevant concepts.
2. Inform participants that you are going to begin by trying to be sure everyone understands the difference between strong boundaries and weak boundaries.
3. Ask for two volunteers for a role-play. Privately read or have volunteers read situation number one. Have volunteers role-play the situation, and ask other participants whether that was an example of weak or strong boundary setting.
4. If time allows, ask for volunteers to role-play situation number three. Since situation number two is of a sexual nature, read that scenario aloud rather than role-playing.
5. If time and interest allows for more role-playing, split group into pairs. Pairs may choose one of the four situations under "Now you practice ..." or make up their own situations for role-plays that demonstrate setting strong boundaries. Allow teens five or ten minutes to develop and practice their role-plays.
6. Reconvene the group and have teens take turns performing their role-plays.
7. Distribute worksheets and instruct participants to fill in the blanks as indicated.
8. Instruct participants to complete the bottom box indicating a boundary they need to set in their own relationships. This may be a relationship with an intimate partner, a parent, a friend, a co-worker or boss, or anyone else.
9. Invite participants to share with the group the areas where they need to set boundaries in their personal relationships, and discuss.

Activity (Individual):
1. Read or have participant read aloud the introductory paragraph, and discuss concepts as necessary.
2. Read or have participant read through and complete each section, processing as necessary.
3. For the final section, suggest a role-play with the teen playing the role of him or her self, and the counselor playing the role of the person he or she wants to set a boundary with. This may be a relationship with an intimate partner, a parent, a friend, a co-worker or boss, or anyone else. Have participant fill in the final line once they are satisfied with the result of the role-play.

ANSWER KEY:
1) strong
2) weak
3) strong

Use In Conjunction With:
SEALS+PLUS, *"Limits,"* (page 19)
SEALS II, *"Developing Boundaries,"* (page 39)
SEALS III, *"Setting Boundaries,"* (page 52)

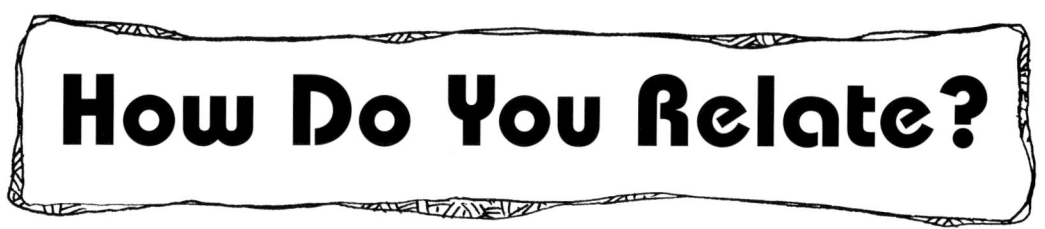

How Do You Relate?

Most people use one of four styles of relating to others: Aggressive, Passive, Passive-Aggressive, or Assertive. Read the descriptions of the four styles and decide — which style do you think is most effective?

An **AGGRESSIVE** person tends to overpower other people. He or she is often loud, bossy and dominating. When confronted with a conflict, this person will often verbally attack the other person. He or she blames other people and is rarely willing to admit responsibility for his or her own part in a conflict. An aggressive person violates other people's rights in order to get what they want. Any use of violence is aggressive behavior.

A **PASSIVE** person tends to avoid dealing with problems and does not speak up for his or her rights. S/he is often nervous or anxious, seems to have little self-confidence, and talks in a quiet voice. This person often tries so hard to please others that s/he doesn't take care of his or her own needs. Because the passive person 'stuffs' anger instead of expressing it, the anger may build up inside. This built-up anger will either lead to an explosion, or the person may develop problems like depression, headaches and other pains, sleeplessness and anxiety.

A **PASSIVE-AGGRESSIVE** person may seem to be passive because they behave quietly and do not directly address conflicts. But instead of 'stuffing' anger, this person will 'get back at' the person they are angry with in a sneaky, underhanded way or in a way that will hurt the other person without drawing attention to him or herself. S/he might even do things unconsciously to hurt the person they are upset with. This person is often suspicious or distrustful of others. Because this person does not address the real problem, s/he rarely gets his or her needs met.

An **ASSERTIVE** person is clear, confident, cool and in control of his or her self at all times. This person stands up for his or her rights without stepping on other people's rights. He or she speaks directly, honestly and respectfully with a clear speaking voice. The assertive person is able to say "no" to something he or she is uncomfortable with, and is not willing to compromise his or her own values or beliefs in order to make another person happy.

Now, see how well you understand the four types of behavior.
Read the following example of a situation between Kendra and Will, then read Kendra's four possible reactions. Write the letter for whether Kendra's style of relating in that example is:
(A) Aggressive (B) Passive (C) Passive-Aggressive or (D) Assertive.

The situation: Will and Kendra made plans to meet at a party at 8:00. The party was given by a friend of Will's. Kendra hardly knew anyone at the party, so she was very uncomfortable being there alone when Will was 45 minutes late.

The responses:

1. When Will shows up, Kendra kisses him hello and acts like nothing is wrong. When Will says "Sorry I was late," Kendra says "It's okay." _____

2. When Will shows up, Kendra says hello and asks to speak with him alone for a minute. She says, "Will, you were 45 minutes late and I was really uncomfortable being here alone because I don't know anyone here. What happened?" She gives him a chance to explain and after Will apologizes she says "I accept your apology, but I don't like to be kept waiting. Next time I want you to call if you're going to be late." _____

3. When Kendra sees Will coming, she starts flirting with another guy, thinking that will teach him not to make her wait. _____

4. When Will shows up, Kendra goes off on him. Before he even gets a chance to say anything, she's yelling at him in front of everyone, "Where the (bleep) were you? Who do you think you are making me wait for you for 45 minutes, you inconsiderate (bleep – bleep)! Now you can forget this party, we're leaving now!" _____

Facilitator's Information for
How Do You Relate?

Purpose: To understand the difference between Aggressive, Passive, Passive-Aggressive and Assertive styles of relating to other people.

Materials: One photocopy of worksheet per participant
Pens/pencils
Additional for GROUP: Flipchart and markers/blackboard and chalk

Activity (Group):
1. On flipchart or board, write the words Aggressive, Passive, Passive-Aggressive and Assertive.
2. Ask group members to define the term 'aggressive' and brainstorm the specific behaviors seen in an aggressive person. After the group has completed brainstorming, read the definition given on the worksheet.
3. Repeat brainstorming and reading definitions for each of the other three terms.
4. Ask for up to eight volunteers for role-plays. If you don't have eight volunteers, two or more volunteers can role-play all of the scenes.
5. Take the volunteers aside and give a copy of the worksheet to each pair, with one or more of the 'Responses' circled. Read 'The Conflict' aloud, and tell each pair they are to role-play the response(s) circled. They may elaborate on the response as much as they want, as long as their role-play still portrays the same style of conflict resolution.
6. Allow five or ten minutes for teens to plan and practice their role-plays.
7. Have each pair perform its role-play for the rest of the group. After each role-play, ask the group to identify which style of conflict resolution was depicted in the role-play.
8. After completing all role-plays, distribute the worksheets and instruct teens to complete the bottom section based on the role-plays that were just performed.
9. Process with the following questions:
   * How did each of Kendra's responses make Will feel?
   * How do you think Will would have reacted to each of Kendra's responses?
   * Based on the above, what is the most effective style of conflict resolution and why?
   * Which styles of conflict resolution does each participant think s/he tends to use?

Activity (Individual):
1. Give teen worksheet and read or have him or her read aloud the introductory paragraph.
2. Ask teen if s/he has any idea what any of the four terms mean, and discuss his/her understanding of the words.
3. Read and discuss the explanations of each of the four styles of relating. For each style, ask participant for examples of that style of relating in his or her own behavior or in behaviors of other people.
4. When the teen thinks s/he understands the concepts of each of the four styles of relating, instruct teen to complete the bottom section or work with teen to match the situations with the styles of relating.
5. Process as in #9 above.

Follow-up Activity: Assert Yourself with "I" Statements, (page 76)

Use In Conjunction With:
SEALS+PLUS, *"Assertion Diary,"* (page 10)
SEALS II, *"We Are People With,"* (page 8)
SEALS III, *"Communication Word Search,"* (page 31)
CROSSING THE BRIDGE, (pages 28, 29, 30)

Assert Yourself With "I" Statements

One way of being assertive is to communicate your feelings and needs directly and honestly, without attacking the other person. The "I" statement is a way of doing this. There are four steps to making an assertive "I" statement.

Step 1: **I feel...**
Make an honest statement about how you are feeling.
For example, "I feel very angry..."
- Hint - make sure you are really stating a feeling, not a thought or a belief about the other person. "I feel you are totally inconsiderate..." is a "You" statement disguised as an "I" statement.

Step 2: **Because...**
Tell the person what action or behavior of theirs has triggered your feelings.
For example, "...because you are 45 minutes late and I've been worried about you."
- Hint - Be specific about why you feel that way, and talk about the present, like in the example above, rather than the past, as in "you're always late."

Step 3: **I want or need...**
Tell the person specifically what you want or need from him or her now or in the future when similar situations arise.
For example, "I need you to be on time next time, and if for some reason you're going to be late I want you to call me."
- Hint - Make your needs or wants reasonable, and make sure you phrase them as your needs, not as demands, as in "you better..." or "next time you will..."

Step 4: **I will...**
This step is optional. Hopefully the other person will give you what you need after step 3. However, if the problem persists, tell the other person what you are prepared to do to respond.
For example, "I won't go out with you the next time you're late."
- Hint - Don't make threats. Think carefully about what you say in this step because if you threaten something that you don't follow through with, you are giving the person the message that you don't mean what you say and your mind can easily be changed.

NOW YOU TRY!
Turn the following "You" Statements into "I" Statements using the four steps.

1. "You are such a lazy slob! I get stuck doing all the work around here! Clean up your mess now and don't ever let me see your dishes in the sink again OR ELSE!"

   I feel _____ because _____

   I want _____ (I will _____)

2. You are totally untrustworthy for telling my secret!

   I feel _____ because _____

   I want _____ (I will _____)

3. You're so loud all the time - why don't you just shut up!

   I feel _____ because _____

   I want _____ (I will _____)

Facilitator's Information for
Assert Yourself With "I" Statements

Purpose: To practice using "I" statements as a technique for assertive communication.

Materials: One photocopy of one worksheet per participant
Pens/pencils

Activity (Group):
1. This activity should be done as a follow-up to How Do You Relate? or another activity introducing the concept of assertiveness. Begin by reviewing that activity and the relevant concepts.
2. Distribute worksheets and pens/pencils. Read or have participants read the introductory paragraph and the 'Four Steps' to assertiveness with their examples.
3. Ask for volunteers to role-play. Pair participants and assign each pair to one of the three examples at the bottom of the page. Instruct them to first develop a role-play based on the original statement, and then develop a second role-play based on an assertive way of handling that same situation using "I" statements. If you have more than three pairs of participants volunteering to role-play, make up additional situations or allow the participants to do so.
4. Allow five or ten minutes for teens to develop and practice their role-plays.
5. Have each pair take turns performing their non-assertive role-plays. Ask 'audience' members to identify which type of behavior (aggressive, passive or passive-aggressive) is being portrayed in the role-play. Then have the participants role-play their assertive way of handling the same situation, or as an alternative, invite audience members to take the place of one or both characters, role-playing assertive conflict resolution using "I" statements.
6. After completing role-plays and processing, distribute worksheets and instruct participants to write in their assertive responses to the bottom section of the worksheet.

Activity (Individual):
1. This activity should be done as a follow-up to How Do You Relate? or another activity introducing the concept of assertiveness. Begin by reviewing that activity and the relevant concepts.
2. Give teen worksheet and read or have him/her read aloud the introductory paragraph.
3. Read and discuss each of the four steps outlined in the worksheet.
4. Instruct participant to turn the non-assertive 'you' statements at the bottom of the page into assertive "I" statements.
5. Ask participant to identify a situation in his/her life in which s/he needed to be more assertive. After processing the situation, ask teen to role-play addressing that situation by using "I" statements. The participant should play him or herself and facilitator should play the role of the person he or she is confronting.
6. Continue formulating and practicing "I" statements until the participant is comfortable with this assertiveness technique. Suggest the teen set a goal to address a problem in his or her life by using "I" statements before the next counseling session, and be sure to follow up at the beginning of the next session.

Use In Conjunction With:
SEALS+PLUS, *"Assertive Rights,"* (page 11)
SEALS II, *"Broken Record Technique,"* (page 3)
SEALS III, *"How to Handle Your Anger,"* (page 59)
CROSSING THE BRIDGE, (pages 28, 29, 30, 31)

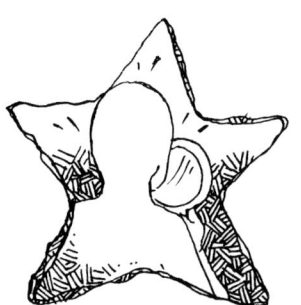

Building Self-Esteem Through Positive Self-Talk

What is Self-Esteem? Self-esteem refers to how you think and feel about yourself. It is your sense of self-worth, your belief about how valuable and worthy a person you are. People with high self-esteem feel good about themselves, and people with low self-esteem feel badly about themselves.

How do we get self-esteem? Self-esteem usually comes from messages you get about yourself. These messages can come from *other people* (like parents, teachers or friends) or from your self. When we get messages from other people that tell us we are 'bad,' we often learn to tell *ourselves* that we are bad or unworthy, and we develop *low* self-esteem. When we get messages from *other people* that tell us we are 'good,' we usually learn to tell *ourselves* that we are good and valuable people, and we develop *high* self-esteem.

What does self-esteem have to do with relationships? The messages we get from people we care about have a very strong affect on our self-esteem. If you are in a healthy relationship, your partner acknowledges your strengths and positive qualities, has confidence in your ability to make good decisions, trusts you and encourages you to pursue your goals. Having a supportive person like this in your life probably makes you feel good about yourself, so your self-esteem improves. If you are in an unhealthy relationship, your partner might put you down, blame you for all of the problems in your relationship, and discourage you from activities that will help you grow as a person. Even if you have high self-esteem when you start your relationship, if you are around an emotionally abusive person for long enough, your self-esteem will eventually get lower.

How can I build my self-esteem? Self-esteem doesn't only come from the messages other people send you – it also comes from the messages you send yourself, called 'Self-Talk'. If you are used to hearing negative messages from other people, chances are you will send yourself negative messages too. Things like "I'm so stupid," "I'm not good enough at this…" or "It's my fault this happened because…" are examples of negative self-talk. One way to build your self-esteem is to re-train yourself to engage in positive self-talk. Positive self-talk is when you focus on your strengths and positive qualities, reminding yourself that you are a good and valuable person.

Some examples of positive self-talk
  "I am a good and caring person and deserve to be treated with respect."
  "I am capable of achieving success in my life."
  "There are people who love me and will be there for me when I need them."
  "I deserve to be happy."
  "I am entitled to make mistakes and to learn from them."

Finish the sentences below:

1. I am a strong person. An example of a time I was strong is _____

2. I am capable of being happy. A time I was happy was _____

3. I am a good friend. A time I was there for a friend was _____

4. I am capable of making decisions for myself. A time I made a good decision was _____

5. I am lovable. People who love me without abusing me are _____

6. I am talented. One thing I am good at is _____

7. _____

Repeat the above sentences to yourself regularly to get in the habit of positive self-talk.

Facilitator's Information for
Building Self-Esteem Through Positive Self-Talk

Purpose: To understand the concept of self-esteem and how it relates to relationships.
To identify personal strengths and practice making self-affirming statements.

Materials: One photocopy of worksheet per participant
Pens/pencils

Activity (Group or Individual):
1. Read or have participant(s) read aloud the four questions and answers, taking time to discuss concepts and terms.
2. Ask participant(s) to volunteer to read the examples of positive self-talk statements (in a group, try to have a different participant read each statement.)
3. Instruct participant(s) to complete the six sentences at the bottom of the page, and to add at least one other self-affirming statement.
4. If working with a group, have participants go around in a circle taking turns repeating each of the positive statements they have written about themselves. If working with an individual, encourage teen to repeat each self-affirming statement several times.
5. Process activity with the following questions and points:
   * How did it feel making positive statements about yourself? It might be awkward at first but it will probably get easier as you get more comfortable with the truth about your positive self.
   * What are times when positive self-talk might be helpful to you?
   * Can anyone give examples of negative self-talk they engage in? Can you turn those negative statements into positive statements about yourself?
   * How could positive self-talk help a person in an abusive relationship?
   * Do you think most people have times when their self-esteem is low?
6. Tell participant(s) that their 'homework' assignment is to repeat their 'Positive Self-Talk' statements aloud, either in a mirror or while sitting quietly with their eyes closed, every day, between now and the next session. Be sure to check in about this experience at the beginning of the next session.

Facilitator's Note: Often a participant will raise the idea that some people's self-esteem is too high, and they act 'conceited'. Point out that often people who feel badly about themselves put on an act in order to hide their bad feelings, and they come off as acting conceited. That kind of behavior is actually often a sign of low self-esteem.

Follow-up Activity: Action Plan for Improving My Self Esteem, (page 80)

Use In Conjunction With:
SEALS+PLUS, *"I Will Like Myself A-Z,"* (page 53)
SEALS II, *"I Am Someone Who,"* (page 58)
SEALS III, *"Self Talk,"* (page 45)
CROSSING THE BRIDGE, (pages 12, 20, 21, 23, 24, 25, 26, 36, 37, 38)

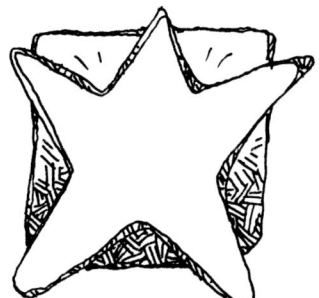

Action Plan for Improving My Self-Esteem

After reading each of the strategies for improving self-esteem, check the ones you plan to use and fill in your personal plan for using these strategies.

☆ Positive self-talk:
I will be aware of my self-talk. I will try not to put myself down, but to put myself up instead, with positive self-talk. Here are some examples of statements I will repeat to myself when I start to feel badly or get the urge to put myself down.

_____
_____
_____

☆ Journaling:
I can use a journal to help me sort out my feelings and to write down positive statements about who I really am (another way of practicing positive self-talk.)

I have a journal __ Yes __ No

If I don't have a journal, here is my plan to get and use one:

_____
_____

☆ Exercise:
Exercise can relieve stress, give me time to think positively about myself, and make me feel good about my health and my body. It does not have to be strenuous, but I will try to exercise at least three times a week. I have written the exercises I can do:

- ☆ Walking on the streets or in a park
- ☆ Riding a bike
- ☆ Working out with weights in a gym
- ☆ Dancing
- ☆ _____

- ☆ Jogging on the streets or in a park
- ☆ Swimming
- ☆ Taking an aerobics class
- ☆ Taking a martial arts class
- ☆ _____

☆ Activities I feel good about:
I will try to put aside some time every day to do something I enjoy, like a hobby or activity I can do on my own. I have checked some of the things I can do, or written in my own activities.

- ☆ Take a walk outside
- ☆ Listen to music
- ☆ Attend a support group
- ☆ Play a sport
- ☆ Make crafts
- ☆ Work out
- ☆ _____

- ☆ Play a musical instrument
- ☆ Write in a journal
- ☆ Participate in a club or after-school group
- ☆ Do volunteer work
- ☆ Meditate
- ☆ _____
- ☆ _____

(continued on next page)

Action Plan For Improving My Self-Esteem (continued)

☆ Assertiveness:
Speaking up for my rights will help others respect me and help me respect myself. I have learned about assertiveness by completing the assertiveness activities in this workbook or in other ways: __ Yes __ No
If yes, here are some of the people and situations I will be more assertive with:

_____

_____

_____

If no, here is how I am going to learn about assertiveness and develop my assertiveness skills:

_____

☆ Increasing Independence:
One way to increase my confidence in myself is to increase my independence - this could be financially, emotionally, socially, physically or in other ways. I will work on becoming more independent in the following areas:

_____

_____

☆ Working with a counselor:
A therapist, counselor or other supportive person can help me to explore any negative self-images I have and turn them into positive ones! This is the person who will work with me on this:

_____

☆ Social life:
Hanging around with people who make me feel good about myself and participating in healthy activities will help me improve my self-esteem.
These are the people I will hang out with: _____
These are the healthy social activities I will participate in with them:

_____

☆ Other:

_____

_____

Facilitator's Information for
Action Plan for Improving My Self-Esteem

Purpose: To identify strategies for improving self-esteem.

Materials: One photocopy of each worksheet per participant
Pens/pencils
Additional for GROUP: Flipchart and Markers/Blackboard and chalk

Activity (Group or Individual):
1. Review previous activity/discussion on the topic of self-esteem, and ask participant(s) to remember one strategy that was discussed for increasing self-esteem (i.e. positive self-talk.)
2. Tell participant(s) that the purpose of today's activity is to come up with additional ways to improve self-esteem.
3. If working with an individual, ask teen if s/he can think of other ways a person might be able to improve his or her self-esteem. Write a list or just facilitate a discussion.
4. If working with a group, brainstorm a list on board or flipchart, or break participants up into smaller groups and ask each group to generate its own list of ways to increase one's self-esteem.
5. After processing list, hand out worksheet(s) and pen(s). Explain that this paper lists some strategies for working on improving self-esteem, and it will allow each participant to make a personalized 'plan' about if and how they want to use each strategy. Point out that if participant(s) came up with strategies that are not on the list, there is room to write them at the bottom.
6. Read or have participant(s) read each strategy, then instruct participant(s) to check the box and fill in the blanks if they think that strategy would be useful to them.
7. As you go along, be sure to point out strategies that are the same or similar as strategies the participant(s) brainstormed.
8. At the end of the page, instruct teen(s) to fill in any other strategies for improving self-esteem that they came up with that are not listed on this page.
9. Suggest each participant set a goal to use at least one of these strategies before the next session. Allow each participant to state which strategy they are going to use, and tell participant(s) that you will check in at the beginning of the next session to see how things worked. (Be sure to follow up during the next session.)

Use In Conjunction With:
SEALS+PLUS, *"Exercise Interest Checklist,"* (page 35)
SEALS II, *"Relationships & You,"* (page 35)
SEALS III, *"Your Picture of Health,"* (page 12)
CROSSING THE BRIDGE, (pages 20, 21, 23, 26, 56, 57)

Let's Talk About Sex

Sex is probably the most controversial and difficult topic to talk about, but one of the most important. Whether or not they are sexually active, everyone should think carefully about their values and decisions about sex because decisions in this area can have some serious consequences. Now of course you know that the only guaranteed way to protect yourself from the consequences of sex is not to do it. But with that said, we're not going to try to tell you what to do — we're only going to suggest that whatever you do, your decision should be a conscious one. Sex doesn't 'just happen.'

TALKING ABOUT SEX (not in the heat of the moment)

Talking about sex with a partner or potential partner can be really awkward. However, it's important to make sure that the decision whether or not to have sex is a decision that is made by both people together — and neither person is being influenced to do something that is not true to their own values about sex.
Below, write the reasons it is important for two people to communicate about sex:

　　Ex: "To make sure it's really what you both want."
___
___
___

Now, write some of the excuses people use to avoid communicating about sex even when they're sexually active:

　　Ex: "I know what s/he wants without having to be told."
___
___
___

Write some suggestions for raising the subject — exactly what words could you use?

　　Ex: "I saw this really deep show on HIV & AIDS yesterday…"
___
___
___

SAYING "NO" TO SEX

Sometimes people want to say no to sex but go along with it anyway. Below, write some of the reasons people might agree to have sex even when they don't want to.

　　Ex: Want the other person to ask them out again
___
___
___

How could you make sure your partner isn't just "going along" with sex when they don't want to?
___
___
___

Below, write as many ways you can think of — verbal and non-verbal — to clearly communicate "No" to sex.

　　Ex: "I like you, but I don't want to have sex."
___
___
___

(continued on next page)

Let's Talk About Sex (continued)

CONSEQUENCES

What are some of the possible physical consequences of sex?

Positive	Negative

Ex: Can feel good if you're in a loving relationship	Ex: Can result in HIV/AIDS
_____	_____
_____	_____
_____	_____
_____	_____

What are some of the possible emotional consequences of sex?

Positive	Negative
_____	_____
_____	_____
_____	_____
_____	_____
_____	_____

What are some of the possible consequences of sex to your relationship?

Positive	Negative
_____	_____
_____	_____
_____	_____
_____	_____
_____	_____

Is there anyone else your decisions about sex could affect besides you and your partner? Who and how?
_____
_____
_____

THINGS TO DO INSTEAD OF SEX

Name as many ways you can think of to have fun, express your feelings and be close with someone other than sex.

Ex: Write them a poem	_____
_____	_____
_____	_____
_____	_____
_____	_____
_____	_____

SEX VALUES

List three values you have developed around the issue of sex. You can try to make sure all of your decisions about sex in the future are based on these values.
_____
_____
_____

Facilitator's Information for
Let's Talk About Sex

Purpose: To develop strategies for making healthy and informed decisions about sex.

Materials: One photocopy of each worksheet per participant
Pens/pencils
Additional for GROUP: Flipchart and markers/blackboard and chalk
Prize or incentive for winning team

Activity (Group:)
1. Distribute worksheets and pens/pencils. Read or have participant read aloud the introductory paragraph.
2. On flipchart or board, write heading "WHY TALK ABOUT SEX." Prompt group members to brainstorm reasons that it is important to communicate about sex with a partner. Write the answers on the board or flipchart and process as you go along. Instruct participants to write the most important reasons in the space provided on their worksheets.
3. Repeat the above process with the following headings: "EXCUSES," "HOW TO RAISE THE SUBJECT," "WHY PEOPLE DON'T SAY NO WHEN THEY WANT TO," "HOW TO BE SURE," "HOW TO SAY NO."
4. Split teens up into three groups. Instruct each group to brainstorm positive and negative consequences for one of the first three questions under the "Consequences" section. Allow five minutes for teens to do so.
5. Reconvene the larger group, and have each small workgroup present its list of consequences to the rest of the group. After processing, instruct members to write in the answers in the spaces provided on their worksheets.
6. Address the last question in this section with the group, and brainstorm a list of people who may be affected by the participants' decisions about sex.
7. Again split the group into the same three smaller workgroups, and frame the next activity as a contest, providing some kind of prize or incentive for the winning group if possible. Tell each group they have exactly five minutes to brainstorm as many "Things to Do Instead of Sex" as they can. The list should include ways to express feelings and be close without having sex (they may include things that include physical closeness, like cuddling, but not sexual acts that stop short of intercourse – this is not an 'everything but' list.)
8. After the groups have developed their lists, have each group present their list and count up the number of ideas each group has. When a group has an idea that is the same as another group's ideas, they cancel each other out so that neither group gets credit for that idea, but the idea should remain on the list. Give the group with the most ideas a prize.
9. Suggest that now or as a follow-up activity, the list of "Things to Do Instead of Having Sex" be made into a poster to be hung in your school or agency, or a flyer to be distributed to students in a health class or event that addresses safe sex.
10. Conclude by instructing each student to write in the space provided at the bottom of the worksheet at least three 'values' they have developed around the issue of sex, around which they can base their future decision-making about sex. Ask members to share these with the group.

Activity (Individual:)
1. Give teen worksheet and pen or pencil, and read or have teen read the introductory paragraph.
2. Read each section and assist teen in answering questions and filling in answers in the spaces provided.
3. Process this activity with discussion about how each of the issues raised in this worksheet apply to the teen's current or past relationships, and how the awareness of these issues may change the way the teen deals with these issues in relationships in the future.

Use In Conjunction With:
SEALS+PLUS, *"Saying "No","* (page 13)
SEALS II, *"Sexual Decision Making,"* (page 62)
SEALS III, *"Communicating with "I" Statements,"* (page 30)

The Relationship BILL of RIGHTS

I hereby declare that I have the following rights in my intimate relationships. I also recognize and respect that all other people are entitled to the same rights at all times.

1. To have and express my own feelings and opinions, whether or not others agree.

2. To make decisions about myself, and to have equal decision-making power in my relationships.

3. To say "no" to physical closeness or any other act that makes me uncomfortable, at any time.

4. To refuse a date at any time.

5. To choose my own friends, and to maintain relationships with those friends.

6. To participate in activities that do not include my boyfriend or girlfriend.

7. To control my own money and other possessions.

8. To live free from fear and abuse.

9. To end a relationship.

10. _____.

Signed _____ Date _____

Facilitator's Information for
Relationship Bill of Rights

Purpose: To identify the rights an individual is entitled to in a relationship.
To understand how practicing those rights can enhance a relationship.

Materials: One photocopy of worksheet per participant
Pens/pencils
Additional for GROUP: Flip chart and markers/blackboard and chalk

Activity (Group):
1. Begin group by asking each participant to complete the following sentence:
   I have the right to _____.
2. Facilitate a discussion exploring the concept of 'rights.' Remind participants that everyone is entitled to certain rights like the rights mentioned during the sentence completion.
3. Ask participants if they think people also have a set of rights in relationships. Prompt participants to brainstorm a list of rights they believe they should have in relationships, and write list on flipchart or board.
4. Distribute worksheets. Read or have participants read each item aloud and discuss. Note whether that item was on the list they brainstormed, and if not, ask group members whether they agree that this right should be included. If there are things on the brainstormed list that are not included on the worksheet, have students write those items in the space provided.
5. Process activity with the following questions:
   * How might being clear on your rights help you to have healthy relationships?
   * Would you discuss these rights with your partner? At what point in the relationship would you do this? How would you raise the subject? What if your partner disagreed with something on the list?
   * Do your rights change as the relationship gets more serious?
   * How do you make sure you also respect your partner's rights?

Activity (Individual):
1. Introduce activity by exploring the concept of 'rights.' Remind the teen that everyone is entitled to certain rights, and ask for some examples. They may have heard of certain children's rights, humanrights or civil rights, or may have been informed about the right to confidentiality in counseling with certain exceptions.
2. Ask teen if s/he thinks people also have a set of rights in relationships. Engage him or her in developing a list of rights s/he believes one should have in a relationship.
3. Give teen the worksheet. Together with the teen, read each item and discuss. Note whether that item was on the list that was brainstormed, and if not, ask whether teen agrees that this right should be included. If there are things on the brainstormed list that are not included on the worksheet, have teen write those items in the space provided.
4. Process activity as in #5 above.

Use In Conjunction With:
SEALS+PLUS, *"Saying "NO","* (page 13)
SEALS II, *"Causes of Stress,"* (page 69)
SEALS III, *"Sticks & Stones,"* (page 53)
CROSSING THE BRIDGE, (pages 33, 49, 50)

Contract With Myself

I, _____, define the following behaviors as abuse. I promise never to commit them or tolerate them in a relationship for any reason:

_____
_____
_____
_____
_____
_____
_____
_____

I define the following behaviors as 'respect' in a relationship. I will try to behave in these respectful ways in my relationships.

_____
_____
_____
_____
_____
_____
_____
_____

If I ever become involved in an abusive relationship, or want to help someone else who I think might be in an abusive relationship, the persons or agencies I will call for help are:

_____ Phone # _____
_____ Phone # _____
_____ Phone # _____
_____ Phone # _____

Signature _____ Date _____

Facilitator's Information for
Contract With Myself

Purpose: To define boundaries of acceptable and unacceptable behavior in one's intimate relationships.

Materials: One photocopy of worksheet per participant
Pens/pencils
Phone numbers for domestic violence hotlines
Additional for GROUP: Flipchart or poster-size paper and markers

Activity (Group or Individual):

1. Introduce activity by telling participant(s) that you would like them to define specifically what they mean when they use the terms 'abuse' and 'respect.'
2. If working with a co-ed group, separate the males and females. Give each group two pieces of flipchart paper or large newsprint, with the words 'Abuse' written on the top of one piece of paper and the word 'Respect' on the other. Same-sex groups may or may not be divided, depending on size and group dynamics.
3. For a single participant or a same-sex group, facilitator can act as recorder; or, ask for a volunteer from each group to write.
4. Instruct participant(s) that they will first have five minutes to brainstorm examples of abuse. Examples should be specific behaviors, for example, 'smacking.' Remind participant(s) that brainstorming means to write down everything that anyone in the group calls out, whether other participants agree with it or not.
5. If there is more than one group, to encourage maximum participation, facilitator may frame this activity as a 'contest' between the two groups to see who can write the most examples or who can come up with examples of the different types of abuse.
6. During brainstorming, facilitator may need to prompt participant(s) to include examples of physical, emotional, verbal, sexual and financial abuse.
7. After brainstorming 'Abuse' is completed, instruct participant(s) to brainstorm examples of 'Respect,' and prompt participant(s) to describe examples of respect around physical, emotional, verbal, sexual and financial relationships.
8. If there is more than one group, bring the larger group back together and ask a volunteer from each group to read their lists aloud and explain anything that needs to be explained. If groups were separated by gender or any other characteristic, process by asking whether both groups had similar or very different ideas of what abuse and respect are, or if they express their ideas differently but have the same general ideas.
9. After reviewing and processing the lists, state that while not everyone will agree with everything on these lists, it is important for everyone to define for themselves what is abusive and what is respectful. That way, when we go into relationships, we are clear on what is acceptable and what is unacceptable.
10. Distribute worksheet(s). Review the concept of a contract, stating that participant(s) are being asked to make a promise to themselves about what behaviors they will accept and which ones they will not accept in an intimate relationship.
11. Instruct participant(s) to fill in their names, then take examples from the lists that were generated and write examples of behaviors they believe are abusive and respectful.
12. Instruct participant(s) to fill in the bottom section with names of people or places they will go to for help if they ever find themselves in an abusive situation. Provide numbers of domestic violence hotlines as optional resources for this section, but also suggest they use the names of counselors, friends, family members or other adults who they trust.
13. Instruct participant(s) to sign and date contract.

Use In Conjunction With:
SEALS+PLUS, *"Self-Esteem Boosters & Busters,"* (page 55)
SEALS II, *"Breaking Down Our Walls,"* (page 41)
SEALS III, *"Friendship Quilt,"* (page 51)

The decision to end a difficult relationship, or to stay and keep trying to make it better, is always a hard one. The purpose of this activity is to help you figure out what's the best move for you.

Below, list every reason you can think of for continuing to work at the relationship, and every reason you can think of to end the relationship.

Reasons to Stay	Reasons to Go
_____	_____
_____	_____
_____	_____
_____	_____
_____	_____
_____	_____
_____	_____
_____	_____
_____	_____
_____	_____

Not every reason you have listed will have equal weight in your decision — go back and put 2 stars next to the reasons that have 'double weight' (or 3 stars for triple weight) in your decision.

Here are some more things to think about if you haven't already. Consider how your relationship has affected the following areas of your life, or your partner's life. Add them to one side or the other of your list, if they apply.

- ☐ Physical health
- ☐ Family
- ☐ Self-esteem
- ☐ Goals in Life
- ☐ Friendships
- ☐ School Attendance / Performance
- ☐ Activities you enjoy
- ☐ Spirituality

You may want to talk over your list with someone you trust, to make sure it is complete and honest.

CHECKPOINT: Are you ready to make a decision about whether to stay or go?

Yes _____ No _____

If yes, what is it?_____

Facilitator's Information for
Should I Stay or Should I Go?

Purpose: To identify reasons for continuing or ending a relationship.

Materials: One photocopy of worksheet per participant
Pens/pencils
Optional: Flipchart and markers/blackboard and chalk

Activity (Group or Individual):
1. Introduce activity by stating that some of the hardest decisions we have to make in life have to do with ending or continuing difficult relationships. Today's activity is aimed at helping people make that decision.
2. If working with a group: On flip chart or board, draw two columns titled "Reasons to Stay" and "Reasons to Go." Ask group to brainstorm every reason they can think of that anyone has ever chosen to stay in a relationship. They do not have to be what the participant considers 'good' reasons and they do not have to be the only reason a person stays, just factors that have influenced a person's decision. Then ask them to do the same for reasons people have decided to end a relationship.
3. Distribute a worksheet and pen or pencil to each participant.
4. Read or have participant(s) read aloud the introductory paragraph and directions for the lists.
5. Instruct participant(s) to develop lists of reasons for continuing or ending their current relationship. If a participant is not currently in a relationship, ask him/her to do the activity based on a past or fictional relationship.
6. After participant(s) have completed lists, read the next paragraph and instruct them to put stars next to items that have more weight in their decision.
7. Read or have participant(s) read the next paragraph and the list of factors to consider, and allow them to add to their lists if necessary.
8. If working with a group: Invite participants to go around and share some of their reasons with each other. If working with an individual, the facilitator should process each of the reasons with the teen.
9. Ask participant(s) if they are ready to make a decision about whether to stay or go. No one should be pressured to end a relationship if they are not ready, even if the facilitator knows the relationship is not healthy – this must be a conclusion the young person comes to on his or her own.
10. Instruct participant(s) to write their decisions in the space provided in the 'checkpoint' box. Tell them you will follow up with an activity about how to end a relationship or what to do if you have decided to stay.
11. Before ending this session, be sure to remind participant(s) that if anyone has decided to end a relationship with a partner who has ever been violent or threatened violence, they should not do so without having a safety plan in place. Breaking up is the most dangerous time of an abusive relationship. In individual work, immediately help the young person to develop a safety plan around breaking up. In group, ask anyone who has decided to end an abusive relationship to talk to you privately at the end of group to make sure they have a safety plan in place.

Follow-up Activities:
Goals for Improving My Relationship (page 91)
Ending a Relationship (page 94)
Safety Plan (page 99)

Use In Conjunction With:
SEALS+PLUS, *"Right to Change,"* (page 12)
SEALS+PLUS, *"Positive Problem Solving,"* (page 44)
SEALS III, *"Hand,"* (page 9)
CROSSING THE BRIDGE, (pages 49, 50, 51)

Goals For Improving My Relationship

If you have decided to stay and work on a relationship that is difficult, even painful or abusive, then it is important to be clear about what needs to change and how you plan to make those changes happen. A couple of things to keep in mind:

- You can not make your partner change. You can let your partner know what changes you need him or her to make, but it is up to your partner to make the changes or not.

- You are not responsible for your partner's actions. If your partner is abusive, changing your behavior will not make the abuse stop.

Start with listing what you've tried that has not worked to improve your relationship in the past.

_____   _____

_____   _____

What are the things that must change in order for you to continue this relationship?

_____   _____

_____   _____

Now set goals for those changes to happen.

Goal 1: _____

Who is responsible for making this goal happen? _____

What are the steps that will need to be taken to achieve this goal? _____

_____   _____

When will I reevaluate this goal to see if it has been achieved? _____

What will happen if the goal is reached? _____

_____

What will happen if the goal is not reached? _____

_____

(continued on next page)

Goals For Improving My Relationship

(continued)

Goal 2: _____

Who is responsible for making this goal happen? _____

What are the steps that will need to be taken to achieve this goal? _____
_____   _____

When will I reevaluate this goal to see if it has been achieved? _____

What will happen if the goal is reached? _____
_____

What will happen if the goal is not reached? _____
_____

Goal 3: _____

Who is responsible for making this goal happen? _____

What are the steps that will need to be taken to achieve this goal? _____
_____   _____

When will I reevaluate this goal to see if it has been achieved? _____

What will happen if the goal is reached? _____
_____

What will happen if the goal is not reached? _____
_____

To add more goals, get another copy of this page or write goals on the back.

Facilitator's Information for
Goals For Improving My Relationship

Purpose: To identify changes that need to occur in one's relationship, who is responsible for making those changes, and how participants will know whether the changes have occurred.

Materials: One photocopy of each worksheet per participant
Pens/pencils

Activity (Group or Individual):
1. Distribute worksheet and pen or pencil to each participant.
2. Read or have participant(s) read aloud the introductory paragraph and "things to keep in mind." Process as needed.
3. Instruct participant(s) to list the things that have not worked to make change in the past, then list the changes that need to be made in order for the relationship to work.
4. Instruct participant(s) to complete at least three "goal plans" for their relationship.
5. If working with a group: Invite participants to share their goals with the group.
6. Process with the following questions:
   * Why does this worksheet say that you can not make your partner change?
   * What is the difficulty with setting goals for your relationship without your partner involved in the goal-planning process?
   * Who did participant(s) write is responsible for making goals happen? Is it all you, all your partner, or both?
   * Do people think they would be comfortable and safe sharing this goal planning process with their partners? What are the conflicts that could come up?
   * How might setting concrete goals like this help to improve your relationship?
   * How can goal-setting be scary?
   * How does a person know when a goal has been reached or not?
   * At what point do you give up trying to make changes if the other person isn't willing to make changes too?

Use In Conjunction With:
SEALS+PLUS, *"Goal Setting,"* (page 29)
SEALS II, *"Good Manners,"* (page 65)
SEALS III, *"Goal Obstacle Plan,"* (page 18)
CROSSING THE BRIDGE, (pages 50, 51)

Ending A Relationship

Ending a relationship is never easy. Your relationship is something you have probably invested a lot of emotional energy in, and it's a letdown that things didn't turn out the way you planned. It might help to remember that you have grown from your experiences in this relationship – even from the most painful parts of it – and what you have learned from this relationship can help to make future relationships more successful. Also remember that you have the <u>right</u> to end a relationship any time you want to.

How do I end the relationship?

That depends. If your partner has <u>ever</u> been violent or threatened violence, even once, then it is very important that you not attempt to break up until you have a safety plan in place. Work with your counselor to complete the <u>Safety Plan</u> in this workbook.

If you have no concerns about your physical safety:

1. First, be clear about your reasons for breaking up, and be sure that ending the relationship is what you want to do. It's normal to feel confused at times, but never tell someone you want to break up with them as a way of manipulating them or getting them to do something you want them to do. Don't say you want to break up if you don't mean it.

    What are your reasons for ending the relationship? _____
    _____
    Are you sure that breaking up is what you want to do? _____

2. Choose a time when you have plenty of time to talk about your reasons for the break-up and for both of you to let out your feelings about it. (However, don't be surprised or angry if your partner does not want to talk about it too much and leaves abruptly. This is his or her way of saying s/he is overwhelmed with emotions and needs some time alone to think about it.)

    This is when I will tell my partner: _____

3. Choose a quiet, private place to let your partner know in person that you want to end the relationship. Don't do it on the phone, through a friend or by letter (unless you are concerned about violence). Even if you're not concerned about violence, it's still a good idea not to be <u>too</u> isolated – be within ear shot of other people just in case things get out of control, but somewhere you can have privacy to talk and cry if necessary.

    This is where I will tell my partner: _____

4. Be clear, honest and 'firm but gentle' when telling your partner you want to end the relationship. Don't be wishy-washy, because it might lead your partner to think he or she can change your mind, and it's unfair to lead someone on like this. But don't be cruel either – there is no reason to put your partner down or try to make them feel bad. Use your assertiveness skills and "I" messages. (Work with your counselor on assertiveness skills if you haven't already.)

    These are the words I will use to let my partner know I want to end the relationship:
    _____
    _____

5. It's OK to agree to be friends, but it's a good idea to limit your time together so you can both have time to process your feelings and move on. And don't be surprised if your partner does not want to be friends – it may be too painful right now to be around you. However, even if you decide you can't be friends, you can still respect the relationship you had by being polite if you run into each other and by not badmouthing your ex.

6. Be prepared to cope with difficult feelings about breaking up, so you don't end up going back to a relationship you really don't want to be in. Work with your counselor to complete the worksheet on <u>Dealing with a Breakup</u>.

Facilitator's Information for
Ending A Relationship

Purpose: To prepare emotionally for ending a relationship, and to develop a plan for ending the relationship in a way that is respectful and healthy for both partners.

Materials: One photocopy of worksheet per participant
Pens/pencils

Activity (Group or Individual):
1. Distribute worksheet and pens/pencils.
2. Read or have participant(s) read aloud the opening two paragraphs.
3. Discuss with participant(s) the idea that ending a violent relationship can be very dangerous. Tell participant(s) that most people who are killed by a partner are killed while breaking up or after the breakup. For this reason, it is important to determine whether participant(s) will be in any danger when or after they tell their partner(s) they want to break up. Participants who have any concerns about their safety should work with facilitator/counselor to complete the Safety Plan before attempting to break up with their partners.
4. If working with a group in which not all participants are considering ending a relationship, suggest they complete the worksheet based on a hypothetical or fictional situation, so they will have 'practice' in case they are ever in the position of having to end a relationship.
5. Instruct participant(s) to read each item and fill in the blank spaces, allowing sufficient time for them to do so and processing with the group afterwards. Or, go over each item on the worksheet as a group and process as you go along.
6. Process with the following questions:
   * The first paragraph of the worksheet says to remember that you have the right to end a relationship any time you want. What does this mean? Why do some people feel like they don't have that right or that their partners don't have that right? When someone thinks their partner doesn't have the right to break up with them, how might they act?
   * What is the concern about safety when someone is breaking up with someone who has been violent in the past?
   * How can you be sure (or can you be sure) that breaking up is what you really want to do?
   * Can you avoid hurting someone when you break up with them?
   * Why is it important to end a relationship in a respectful way?
   * What are some of the times and places people decided they would end a relationship?
   * What are some of the words people would use to end a relationship?

Follow-up Activity: Dealing With a Breakup, (page 97)

Use In Conjunction With:
SEALS+PLUS, *"Limits,"* (page 19)
SEALS II, *"Set the Stage,"* (page 6)
SEALS III, *"What do I Want to Change,"* (page 41)
CROSSING THE BRIDGE, (pages 49, 51)

Dealing With A Breakup

If you've decided to end a relationship, it's a good idea to be prepared for your partner's reaction as well as your own feelings.

How will my partner react when I end the relationship?

There's no way to be sure, but below are some common and pretty normal reactions to a break up. Are you prepared for them? Write how you will respond to each of the following reactions by your partner.

- Disbelief, even if you think your partner should have seen it coming _____
- Crying _____
- Some degree of anger directed towards you, but no violence or threats _____
- Acting as if he or she doesn't care _____
- Making some effort to get you to change your mind, but without threats or coercion _____
- Denying that it is really over by saying that he or she believes that you'll get back together someday – but without making scary threats _____
- Trying to hurt you back by saying mean things _____
- Wanting a detailed reason for the breakup, and having a hard time accepting the reason you give _____
- Other _____

Most of these reactions are using defense mechanisms – ways of protecting oneself from hurt feelings. The best way to deal with it is to just let your partner use whatever defenses s/he needs to protect him or herself at this time. Your partner's anger at you will probably go away with time. In the mean time, you should have someone you trust to talk to about your feelings.

Below are reactions to a breakup that are NOT normal or acceptable and require you to get HELP from a trusted adult or the police. Write how you will respond if your partner reacts in the following ways. If you think your partner might react in any of these ways, you should have a safety plan in place before breaking up.

- Any violence or threats of violence _____
- Words that scare you like "I will never let you go" or "If I can't have you no one can" _____
- Threats of suicide, stated clearly like "I'll kill myself if you leave me" or implied like "I can't go on living without you" _____
- Refusing to 'let you' breakup by not letting you leave, or refusing to leave you alone _____
- Stalking you after the breakup: following you, calling constantly, or having you watched _____
- Other _____

(continued on next page)

Dealing With A Breakup (continued)

How Will I Feel After the Breakup?

Below are some normal feelings you may experience, along with suggestions for how to deal with them:

- Sadness and frequent crying, but this should begin to slow down after a week or two. It's OK to let yourself be sad and cry – even though you wanted the breakup, you are experiencing a real loss. One healthy way to work through your confusing feelings is to write about them in a journal. Start here by writing some of the feelings you are having while thinking about breaking up: _____
_____
_____

- Feelings of loneliness and missing your partner. You should let yourself go through some of these feelings, but don't sit around feeling lonely for too long. Now is the time to re-connect with your friends and family, get involved in extracurricular activities, or get involved with a project or hobby. Write names of people or activities that can help you cope with the loneliness: _____
_____

- Guilt. There's no way to get around someone getting hurt when a relationship ends. You and your partner will both get through it and grow from the experience. Console yourself by knowing that you did the best thing for your partner by being honest and ending the relationship at the right time; it would have hurt your partner more to string him or her along. Write this sentence in the space below, and remind yourself whenever necessary:
"I have the right to end a relationship. I am making the best decision for me." _____
_____

- Questioning yourself about whether you did the right thing. It is normal to have some doubts, but it is not a good idea to call up your partner and tell him or her about them. This might give your partner false hope and hurt them more, or lead you both into a painful 'on again - off again' cycle. The best thing is to talk about these doubts with someone in your support system, and remind yourself of all of the reasons you made the decision to break up in the first place.
  Who will you talk to? _____
  What are the biggest reasons for your decision to end the relationship? _____
  _____

- Other _____

Below are some more serious reactions to a breakup that you could experience. These reactions mean that you need help from a counselor or doctor. List the people or organizations you will go to for help if you experience each problem:

- Feelings of extreme depression and loneliness that do not go away after a short period _____
_____

- Thoughts about hurting or killing yourself _____
_____

- Loss or gain of more than a few pounds _____
_____

- Use of drugs or alcohol as a way of dealing with the pain _____
_____

- Other _____
_____

Facilitator's Information for
Dealing With A Breakup

Purpose: To help prepare emotionally for ending a relationship.
To plan safe and healthy responses to a partner's reactions and one's own feelings following a breakup.

Materials: One photocopy of each worksheet per participant
Pens/pencils
Flipchart and markers/blackboard and chalk

Activity (Group or Individual):

1. Introduce activity by reviewing past activities on ending relationships. Remind participant(s) that even when the decision is clearly the right one, it is still often very difficult to deal with. The purpose of today's activity is to prepare emotionally for the breakup.
2. On a flipchart or board, write the sentence, "How will my partner react?" Engage teen(s) in brainstorming a list of possible ways a person might react when their partner tells them they want to break up.
3. After generating the list, ask one or more teens to circle the 'normal and safe' reactions on the list (using a green marker if possible,) and circle the reactions that are 'unsafe, unhealthy or abusive' (in red.)
4. Distribute first worksheet and pen or pencil to each participant.
5. Read or have participant(s) read aloud the introductory paragraph and heading to "How will my partner react . . . ?"
6. Either give participant(s) time to fill in the first section on their own, or go over each item aloud and process as you go along. Encourage teen(s) to include any items on their brainstormed list that are not on this worksheet in the space provided.
7. Read or have participant(s) read aloud the paragraph about defense mechanisms following this section. Discuss the concept of defense mechanisms as necessary.
8. Read or have participant(s) read aloud the next paragraph about reactions that are not normal or acceptable, and give teen(s) time to fill in the blanks or go over each item together, again including items on their brainstormed list in the space provided.
9. On flipchart or board, prompt teen(s) to generate another list under the heading "How will I feel after the breakup?" Encourage them to list both positive and negative feelings, reminding them that it is normal to have a mixture of both.
10. After the list is completed, again ask one or more teens to circle the healthy responses in green and the unhealthy ones in red. Review each item on the list and ask teen(s) if they can think of strategies for dealing with each of the feelings and reactions named.
11. Distribute second worksheet for this activity. Read or have participant(s) read aloud the introductory paragraph.
12. Read or have participant(s) read aloud each item, and allow time for teen(s) to write in the spaces provided as each item instructs.
13. Read or have participant(s) read paragraph heading the list of 'more serious' reactions that would require a person to seek help. Allow time for teen(s) to fill in the people or organizations they would go to for each problem.
14. Encourage teen(s) to write in additional feelings and strategies on this worksheet or on a separate piece of paper to attach to this one.

Use In Conjunction With:
SEALS+PLUS, *"Decision Making,"* (page 45)
SEALS II, *"What Have I Been Up To,"* (page 18)
SEALS III, *"Are You Stuck in the Cycle of Fear,"* (page 13)

Safety Plan

SECTION A: If you have decided to stay in a relationship that has been violent in the past

If your partner has been violent in the past, chances are very good it will happen again — even if your partner promised it wouldn't. You may not want to think about that possibility, but for your own safety, it's best to be prepared just in case. Remember, you do not have control over your partner's violence, but you do have control over how you prepare for it and respond to it.

1. These are the 'cues' I have seen in the past right before my partner has been violent. I can keep these in mind as warning signs, and when I see these things in the future I will know it is time to take action to protect myself:
   ___ Use of drugs/alcohol   ___ Jealousy   ___ Verbal abuse/put-downs
   ___ Embarrassing me in front of friends   ___ Disagreements about sex
   _____   _____   _____

2. These are some of the ways I have tried to protect myself in the past that HAVE worked. In the future, as soon as I sense that my partner may become violent, I will do as many of these things as I can to protect myself:
   _____
   _____

3. These are some of the ways I have tried to protect myself in the past that HAVE NOT worked. I will not rely on these things in the future:
   _____
   _____

4. When I sense there is going to be an argument, I will try to go to a place where other people might hear the arguing, and/or a place where there is less risk of injury. (Avoid kitchens, bathrooms, garage, anywhere near weapons or any room without an outside exit.)
   These are the places I will try to avoid having an argument:
   _____
   _____

5. These are the numbers I can call for help when I sense that I'm in danger:
   (Always have these numbers and change for phone calls on you.)
   Police: _____   Under what circumstances will I call? _____
   Hotline: _____   Under what circumstances will I call? _____

   (continued on next page)

100

© 2001 Wellness Reproductions and Publishing, Inc. 800 / 669-9208

Safety Plan (continued)

6. These are the people I can turn to for help who are willing to be a part of my safety plan:

   <u>Name</u>   <u>How they will help</u>

   At home: _____   _____

   At school: _____   _____

   At work: _____   _____

   Around the neighborhood: _____   _____

   Other: _____   _____

7. This is the code word I will use to let the people above know I am in danger and need help: _____

8. If I need to get out of the house quickly when I am in danger, this is how I will escape:
   (Plan as many escape routes as possible, including using doors, windows, fire escapes, elevators, stairwells, etc. Practice the escape route.)
   _____
   _____

9. If I need to go to a safe location where my partner will not find me, this is where I will go:
   _____
   _____

10. I may be able to get a certain type of order of protection that does not require my partner to stay away from me, but does order him or her not to abuse me. This way, my partner knows there will be more serious consequences if s/he is abusive. This is who can help me get the order of protection:
    _____
    _____

11. If I get the order of protection, I should carry a copy on me at all times and have copies at my home, school, work and anyplace else I am likely to be. This is where I will keep copies of my order of protection (or who will hold them for me.)
    _____
    _____

12. If I need medical care, this is where I will go: _____
    This is how I will get there: _____
    My insurance/Medicaid information or how I will pay for it: _____

13. These are some ways I can increase my independence so I will be better prepared to make it on my own if I decide to end this relationship in the future:
    (I can become more independent financially, emotionally, socially, physically, etc.)
    _____
    _____

(continued on next page)

Safety Plan (continued)

SECTION B: If you have decided to break up with an abusive partner

If you are in an abusive relationship – if your partner has ever been violent or threatened violence – it is very important to have a well-planned safety plan in place before attempting to end the relationship. While ending the relationship now is probably the best decision for you in the long run, you should know that the breakup period is the most dangerous time in an abusive relationship.

1. I will plan the breakup carefully with the help of people I trust. If possible, I will involve a parent and a counselor from a local domestic violence services organization. I can also involve friends, counselors, teachers – the more people who are aware of what's going on, the more people can look out for me and support me.
   This is who will help me to carry out my breakup safety plan:
   _____

2. Getting an order of protection is highly recommended if I think I might be in any danger. It is not a guarantee of safety, but it is a legal court order that says my ex-partner must stay away from me and can be arrested if he or she does not. This may scare my ex into leaving me alone. (See the worksheet on Orders of Protection, or ask a domestic violence services agency for help.)
   This is where I can go to get an order of protection:
   _____

3. I will not break up with my partner in an isolated place. I will do it in public, with people around who are a part of my safety plan and know what's going on. If necessary for safety reasons, I will do it by phone or by letter.
   This is where and when I will break up with my partner: _____
   This is who will be around when I do it: _____

4. I will be very clear with my partner that I am ending the relationship and that my decision is not negotiable.
   These are the words I will use: _____
   _____

5. I will be prepared for my partner's reaction. It could be violent, or my partner could be very sweet and try to win me back.
   Ways my partner might react: How I will handle these reactions:
   _____   _____
   _____   _____
   _____   _____
   _____   _____

6. After breaking up, I will avoid being alone with my ex-partner or being in a situation where s/he might try to corner me. I can change my routines, change my travel routes, ask a friend or family member to travel with me to school or work. I will try not to go out alone, especially at night. I should never open the door if my ex comes knocking, no matter how sweet or apologetic s/he sounds.
   These are the routines I will have to change: _____

   These are the people who are willing to travel with me: _____

   This is what I will do if my ex shows up at my home: _____

(continued on next page)

Safety Plan (continued)

Section C: If you are breaking up with an abusive partner who you live with
Breaking up with someone you live with is even more complicated.
Aside from following all of the steps in section B, take the extra precautions below before breaking up.

1. A safe place I can stay, (preferably one where my partner will not find me) is:
   (If necessary get information about how to access a shelter from your local domestic violence hotline)
   _____

2. If I am going to move back in with a parent or stay with a family member or friend where my partner can find me, I will make sure that everyone living in the household is a part of my safety plan.

3. I should get any important personal possessions, identification, documents, money, etc., out of my home. Going back for them could be dangerous, or my partner could try to control me by destroying or 'holding hostage' things that I need.
   These are the things I will remove from the home: _____
   _____
   This is where I will keep them: _____

4. If I plan to stay where I live now and ask my partner to leave, I should change the locks so my partner doesn't have access to the home. (I should do this before I break up or immediately after, and won't stay home alone until the locks are changed.)
   This is the name and number of the locksmith I will use, and how I will pay for it:
   _____

5. If I plan to stay where I live now, I will not allow my ex-partner in the home when I'm alone to get his or her belongings. I will have my partner get his or her things when I'm not home. If I have an order of protection, I can request police be present when my partner picks up his/her things.
   This is when and how I will stay safe when my partner gets his or her belongings:
   _____

SECTION D: If you have a child or children with your abuser
If you have a child or children with your abuser, your safety plan will also have to include making sure your children are safe physically and emotionally. In addition to the precautions above, make sure you do the following things for the safety of your children:

1. This is where I can get counseling for my child(ren) and advice on how to help them deal with the emotional effects of witnessing the violence: _____
   _____

2. I will call the police or child welfare services if my partner abuses my child(ren). (I am responsible for protecting my child(ren), and if my partner hurts them and I fail to seek help, I could be charged with neglect and the child(ren) could be taken away.)

3. If my child(ren) are old enough, I can teach them how to use the phone to call the police or fire department. (If I have a programmable phone, I can program these numbers on speed dial and teach the child(ren) when and how to use them.)

4. If my child(ren) are old enough, I can teach them the escape plan in case they feel they are in danger.

5. I will let anyone who cares for my child(ren) know who else has permission to visit or pick the child(ren) up. If I have an order of protection that includes the child(ren), I will make sure the school, day care or sitters have copies.

Facilitator's Information for
Safety Plan

Purpose: To develop a plan for increased safety while in an abusive relationship or while and after ending one.

Materials: One photocopy of each worksheet per participant
Pens/pencils

Activity (Group or Individual):

1. Introduce activity by stating that while no one is in control of his or her partner's violence, it is possible to plan for how you are going to respond to violence or the threat of violence in as safe a way as possible.
2. Give each participant a worksheet and pen or pencil
3. Read or have participant read the first paragraph aloud.
4. If working with a group where not everyone is in an abusive relationship, suggest that everyone complete the safety plan in case they someday find themselves in a dangerous relationship. It can also help them to be aware of the concept of safety planning in case they someday have a friend or relative in an abusive relationship who needs help.
5. Review each item and discuss possible responses with participant(s). Instruct participant(s) to write in their responses in the space provided.
6. Discuss where participant(s) will keep the written safety plan (aside from putting a copy in their workbooks.) It is a good idea to have it somewhere they have access to, but it may not be safe to keep it with them or at home if there is a chance the abuser might find it. What is important is that they are clear in their mind(s) what they will do if they are in danger.
7. Process this activity with the following questions/points:
   * Does this activity make participant(s) feel better prepared to deal with the possibility of current or future violence?
   * What can the role of parents or guardians be in safety planning? Who are the other people who can have a role in the safety plan?
   * While the safety plan can be helpful, it is not a guarantee of safety. What are some of the other concerns around safety?
8. Be sure to process individually with any participant who is in an actively abusive relationship in order to be sure their safety plan will be as effective as possible.

Use In Conjunction With:
SEALS+PLUS, "*I Love Me,*" (page 56)
SEALS II, *"Safe Place,"* (page 32)
SEALS III, *"HELP,"* (page 79)

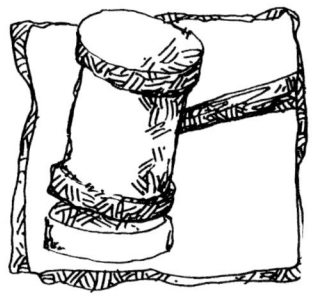
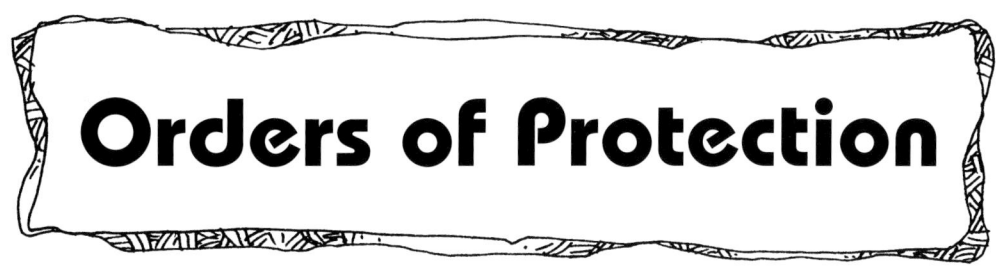

Orders of Protection

Getting an Order of Protection (or Protective Order) is one step you can take to try to put a stop to abuse or harassment. It is not a guarantee of safety, but it can send a serious message to your abuser that you are not willing to put up with abuse.

What is an Order of Protection?
It is a legal order from a judge that sets strong limits on the abuser's contact with you. Every state is different, but in many states an order of protection can do the following things:
- ☆ Order the abuser to stay away from you. It may say the abuser can not come within a certain distance of you, your family, your home, your job or your school. It may also say the abuser can not call you, send you mail or write you notes.
- ☆ Order the abuser not to abuse you. Some types of orders of protection do not make the abuser stay away from you, but say the abuser can not physically hurt you or verbally abuse you.
- ☆ Order the abuser to move out if you live together. You can even request that a police officer come to your home when the abuser comes to get his/her personal belongings.
- ☆ Order the abuser to join a counseling or educational program for abusers.
- ☆ Give you temporary custody of any children you have with the abuser, and order that visits with the children be supervised by a social worker if the children have also been abused.

How do I get an Order of Protection?
You have to apply for an order of protection in court - Family, Criminal or Supreme Court, depending on the situation. Usually, you can go to family court if you are/were married or have a child together. Otherwise you will have to go to criminal or supreme court. Here are some steps you should take:
- ☆ Notify the police during or immediately after an incident of abuse or harassment. This will help build your case in court. If police are involved, write the names of the responding officers here:
  _____
- ☆ Gather evidence of the abuse. Have a friend take a picture if you have any injuries, and get written statements from any witnesses.
  List evidence here: _____
  _____
- ☆ Call a domestic violence or victim advocate agency to get advice. Many agencies have legal counselors who can tell you the specifics about orders of protection in your state, tell you which court to go to, accompany you to court, and provide free legal representation if necessary. If you are a minor, they can also tell you whether you have to have a parent involved in order to get the order of protection.
  The agency you can call and its phone number:_____
- ☆ Complete the forms and file for the order of protection at the appropriate court. You will have to write down details of the abuse, with dates and places. A counselor from the domestic violence services agency or the court clerk can help you. An emergency order of protection can be put in place immediately, and you will be given a hearing date. Write the locations of your local Family, Criminal and Supreme Courts here:
  Family Court: _____
  Criminal Court: _____
  Supreme Court: _____
- ☆ Go to the court hearing and tell your story to the judge. Be sure to have a supportive person with you. The abuser will probably be there and may try to upset or intimidate you. Make sure you get a certified copy of your order of protection.

After getting an Order of Protection:
- ☆ Carry a copy of the order of protection with you at all times.
- ☆ If the abuser violates the order, report it to the police immediately.
- ☆ Do not make contact with the abuser.
- ☆ **<u>Continue to follow your safety plan.</u>** There are risks involved in getting an order of protection because it may make the abuser angry and more dangerous. Even though the abuser can be arrested if s/he violates the order, the abuser may still try to hurt you.

Facilitator's Information for
Orders of Protection

Purpose: To become familiar with the concept of Orders of Protection and develop a plan for getting one if necessary.

Materials: One photocopy of worksheet per participant
Pens/pencils
Phone numbers of local domestic violence services and/or crime victim's advocacy agencies
Addresses of Criminal, Family and Supreme Courts
Literature on how to obtain an order of protection in your state, if available

Activity (Group):
1. If possible, arrange for a speaker to attend the meeting and give a presentation on obtaining orders of protection in your area. Many domestic violence services agencies have legal assistance counselors who will do this.
2. If it is not possible to get a speaker, gather information on obtaining orders of protection from your area's domestic violence services agencies, crime victim's advocacy organizations, court clerk, etc.
3. Distribute worksheets and pens or pencils and review each point with the group, filling in the specifics for your area as necessary. Have participants fill in the blanks in the spaces provided when applicable. Remind them that they can keep these worksheets to use in the future if they ever decide to seek an order of protection.
4. Process with the following questions:
   * What are some of the emotions that might come along with the decision to get an order of protection against a partner or ex-partner? (Common emotions include guilt, relief, fear of partner's reaction, a sense of justice, feelings of loss, feelings of safety...)
   * What are some of the risks involved in getting an order of protection?
   * How do you think abusers might react when they are served with an order of protection?
   * Under what specific circumstances would you seek an order of protection?

Activity (Individual):
1. Gather as much information as possible on obtaining orders of protection from your area's domestic violence services agencies, crime victim's advocacy organizations, court clerk, etc.
2. Review each point on the worksheet with the teen, filling in the specifics for your area as necessary. Have teen fill in the blanks in the spaces provided when applicable. Remind him or her that s/he can keep the worksheets to use in the future if s/he ever decides to seek an order of protection.
3. Process as in #4 above.

Use In Conjunction With:
SEALS+PLUS, *"Procrastination,"* (page 70)
SEALS II, *"A Plan For Staying Alive,"* (page 76)
SEALS III, *"HELP:,"* (page 79)

Is My Relationship Ready for a Baby? Am I?

People choose to have children for a number of reasons, and it is important to be clear about what those reasons are before making that decision. The purpose of this activity is to get you thinking about how ready you and your partner are for a baby.

1. Are you ready for a lifelong commitment to your partner? Even if you break up, a child means a permanent relationship as co-parents. On a scale of 1-10, how certain are you that you want to have a relationship with this person for at least the next 18 years?

(not very certain) 1 2 3 4 5 6 7 8 9 10 **(very certain)**

2. Do you think having a child will change your relationship? List the changes you expect.

Positive Changes   Negative Changes

_____   _____
_____   _____
_____   _____
_____   _____
_____   _____

3. Having a child is sure to be the greatest source of conflict in your relationship. If you have experienced any form of abuse in your current relationship (physical, emotional or sexual) it is most likely that that abuse will escalate (get worse) during pregnancy and when you have a child. In other words, an emotionally abusive relationship often escalates into physical abuse during pregnancy; a physically abusive relationship often gets even more violent, more often.

What's the worst conflict or abuse you've ever experienced with your partner?

_____

What would it look like if the conflict or abuse were twice as bad?

_____

Are you concerned that your child might be affected by violence between you and your partner?

_____

(continued on next page)

Is My Relationship Ready for a Baby? Am I? (continued)

4. Think about your reasons for wanting to have a baby. Many people want to have a baby to fill in something that's missing in their own life or their own relationship - they want to feel loved or have someone to love, or they think caring for a baby will make them feel like a capable adult. When you think about being a parent, what are the most positive ways you imagine it will make you feel?

   _____

   Are there other ways, besides having a baby, you could get to have those feelings?

   _____

   What are the most negative ways you imagine it will make you feel?

   _____

   How will you cope with those feelings when they arise?

   _____

5. List some of your goals in life around school, career, family, social life.

   _____

   _____

   _____

   _____

   How do you think having a baby will affect those goals?

   _____

   _____

   _____

   _____

CHECKPOINT:

Based on your thoughts answering the last five questions, do you think you are ready to have a baby now?   __ Yes   __ No

If yes, go on to the next page for issues to discuss with your partner before making a final decision.

Facilitator's Information for
Is My Relationship Ready for a Baby? Am I?

Purpose: To explore fantasies vs. realities of teen parenting and encourage participants to make responsible decisions about family planning.

Materials: One photocopy of each worksheet per participant
Pens/pencils

Activity (Group or Individual):

1. Distribute worksheet and read or have participant(s) read introductory paragraph.

2. Instruct participant(s) to complete the five questions, allowing ample time to do so and providing assistance with terms and concepts as needed. Worksheets should be completed in pencil because participant(s) will have the opportunity to change their answers during later discussion.

3. After participant(s) have completed the five questions, facilitate a discussion about each question. Use the following suggested discussion points for addressing the 'realities' of teen parenting:

    Question 1: The reality is...no matter what the good intentions of the father, teen moms usually wind up being solely or mostly responsible for their children. No matter how much you love each other now, people's feelings and beliefs change as they grow. Think of it this way: more than half of all marriages end in divorce, and those are mostly adult marriages - it is much less likely for a teen couple to stay together because teens are still growing into their personalities. Ask teens if they have ever had a friend who they were sure would be their best friend forever, but who they later grew apart from.

    Question 2: The reality is...having a baby puts tremendous stress on a relationship. A good guideline is to never go into a marriage or parenthood expecting the other person to change the things you dislike about them. A good assignment for young people is to ask them to interview three to five parents with children over one year of age, and ask them how their relationships changed for better and for worse after they had the baby.

    Question 3: The reality is...pregnancy is much more likely to make abuse worse than to make it better. In one study, 26 percent of pregnant teens reported being physically abused by their partner, and 40-60 percent said the battering had begun or escalated since their boyfriends knew they were pregnant.[1]

    Question 4: The reality is... babies don't give, they take, take, and take. While you will probably love your child a great deal, if you are not in a healthy relationship and prepared in many other ways to be a parent, your baby will probably bring you a lot more frustration than you think. You can not expect a baby to fill something that's missing in you or in your relationship, and it would be very unfair to put all of that on a child. The most loving thing you can do is to resolve those issues for yourself before bringing a baby into the world.

    Question 5: The reality is...even with the best intentions, teen parents have a very high drop-out rate from school, and are much more likely to have to put on hold their dreams of college, career, etc. If you have to give up your dreams, you might wind up resenting your baby and your partner for it. You will be a better parent once you have achieved some of your other goals.

4. After discussion, allow students to add to or change their answers. Then ask them to complete the "checkpoint" box at the bottom of the page.

Follow-Up Activity: For My Partner and Me: Decisions About Having A Baby (page 110)

Use In Conjunction With:
SEALS+PLUS, *"Decision Making,"* (page 45)
SEALS II, *"Life Choices . . . Baby Time Or Not,"* (page 46)
SEALS III, *"Mindfulness Inventory,"* (page 60)
CROSSING THE BRIDGE, (page 33)

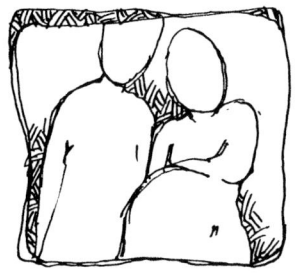

For My Partner & Me: Decisions About Having a Baby

Following are some things you should discuss with your partner before making a decision about having a baby. Once you have discussed and resolved each issue, write down what you and your partner have agreed upon.

1. Have you both been tested for HIV and other Sexually Transmitted Diseases recently, to make sure you don't pass anything on to your baby? _____
2. If either of you use drugs and/or alcohol, are you prepared to stop using while you are trying to get pregnant and during pregnancy? _____
   Will your partner also stop using? _____
   Will you and your partner use drugs/alcohol when you have a child? _____
3. Have you both talked with a health care provider to make sure you can have a healthy baby? _____
   Have you reviewed both your families' medical histories? _____
4. If you/your partner get(s) pregnant, how will you both react to you/your partner gaining weight? _____
5. Are you/your partner prepared for the pain of childbirth? _____
   Have you and your partner seen a video on childbirth so you can understand what is involved? _____
6. How will you support your child financially: Will you and your partner both work, will you receive public assistance, depend on family? _____
7. Who will take care of the baby if you both plan to work? _____
8. If you and your partner break up, will one of you be able to support the baby by yourself if necessary? _____
9. Do you and your partner have the emotional support of your families? _____
   Will they offer support in the way of money or childcare if needed? _____
10. Will you have enough money for food, clothes, diapers, childcare, emergencies, illnesses? _____
11. How will you both feel about changing dirty diapers? _____
12. How will you both react if the baby won't stop crying? _____
13. How will you discipline your child? _____
    Will you ever hit the child? _____
14. How will you feel if your child is born with a disability? _____
15. Are you both prepared to be responsible for a baby 24/7? _____
16. Are you prepared to give up your social life - going out with friends, parties, dates, etc.? _____
17. Will you live together? _____
    If not, how often will each partner care for the child? _____
    If so, who will get up in the middle of the night to feed or change the baby? _____
    Who will do the chores like laundry, cooking, cleaning, etc.? _____
18. _____

Facilitator's Information for
For My Partner & Me: Decisions About Having a Baby

Purpose: To evaluate preparedness for pregnancy and parenting.

Materials: Two photocopies of worksheet per participant
Pens/pencils

Activity (Group or Individual):
1. Hand out worksheet and read or have participant(s) read aloud the introductory paragraph.
2. Read or have participant(s) read aloud each question. After each question, ask teens(s) whether they have discussed this issue with their partner or already done this thing. Facilitate discussion about why each issue is important, invite teen(s) to share experiences around these issues, and ask whether they think their partner(s) will agree with them on these issues. Instruct participant(s) to write their own answers in the spaces provided.
3. After reviewing and discussing the entire worksheet, give participant(s) another copy of the worksheet. Tell them that they may, if they feel comfortable and safe doing so, share the worksheet with their partner(s). They and their partner(s) may either work on completing the worksheet together, or the participant may ask his or her partner to complete it alone, then compare answers to see how close their thinking is on these issues.
4. Follow up during the next session with a discussion of why participant(s) did or did not share the worksheet with their partner(s), and what they learned about the communication patterns of their relationship.

Use In Conjunction With:
SEALS+PLUS, *"One Step at a Time,"* (page 32)
SEALS II, *"Life Choices... Baby Time Or Not,"* (page 46)
SEALS II, *"ABCD's of Self-Parenting,"* (page 45)

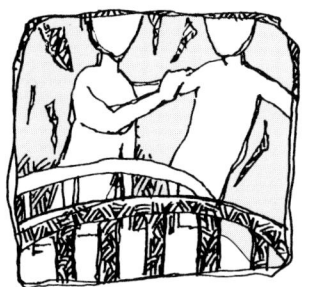

The Effects of Relationship Abuse on Children

If you are in an abusive relationship and have children or are thinking about having a baby, there are some things you should know about how your relationship will affect your child. First of all, your child is much more likely to be abused him or herself. About 70% of men who abuse their female partners also abuse their children.[1] Even if your partner doesn't abuse your child, the emotional effects of being in an abusive relationship might make YOU more likely to abuse or neglect your child.

Here are just some of the characteristics that are common among children who witness relationship abuse (see or hear the abuse, or see the aftereffects of the abuse.)

Many children who witness relationship abuse[2]:

- Suffer from depression, sadness, stress and anger
- Refuse to go to school
- Act out sexually (are very promiscuous or sexually abusive)
- Run away
- Suffer from low self-esteem and have few expectations for success
- Have troubled relationships with peers
- Are in constant fear for their own lives or their parents' lives
- Lie, cheat and steal
- Believe that violence is normal
- Begin hitting as a way of solving problems at a very young age
- Become involved in abusive relationships as teens
- Use violence in school, with peers and with family members
- Are at risk for suicide
- Have thoughts of murdering their parents
- Feel constantly confused and insecure

Children who witness relationship abuse are affected in these ways because they learn certain things from their environment. Below are some of the things children learn from violence. Next to each item, write what you want to teach your children.

What Violence Often Teaches Children...

It's OK to hurt others in order to control them

They should be ashamed of their families

They are powerless and incompetent
   (which leads to low self-esteem)

People can not be trusted

The world is a scary place, it is never safe

Love and violence go together

Males are cruel, controlling and violent*

Females are weak and powerless*

*(If they are witnessing male on female violence)

What I Want to Teach my Children by Role-Modeling Healthy Relationships...

_____
_____
_____
_____
_____
_____
_____
_____
_____

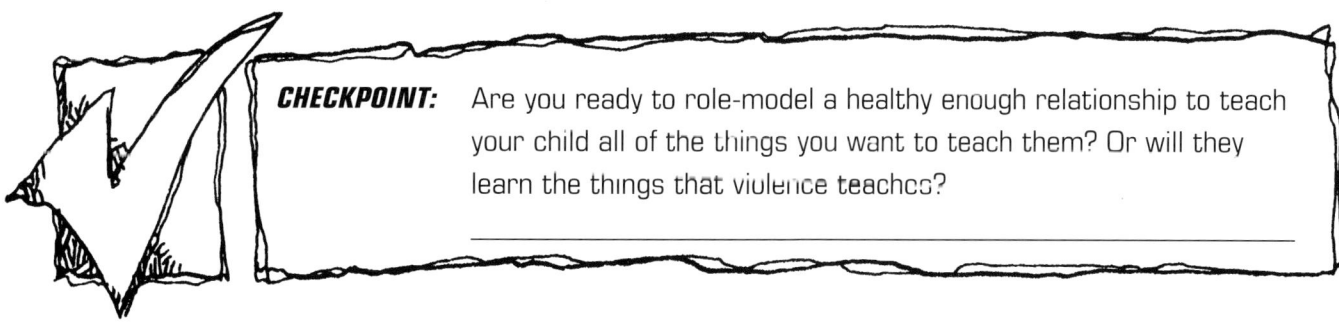

CHECKPOINT: Are you ready to role-model a healthy enough relationship to teach your child all of the things you want to teach them? Or will they learn the things that violence teaches?

_____

Facilitator's Information for
The Effects of Relationship Abuse on Children

Purpose: To understand some of the effects relationship abuse has on children.

To identify values that participants want to teach their own children about relationships.

Materials: One photocopy of worksheet per participant
Pens/pencils

Activity (Group or Individual):
1. Distribute worksheet(s) and pens/pencils.
2. Read or have participant(s) read aloud the introductory paragraph, followed by the list of characteristics of children who witness relationship abuse. Discuss as necessary.
3. Read or have participant(s) read next paragraph and "What Violence Often Teaches Children." Discuss as necessary.
4. Allow participant(s) five or ten minutes to develop a list of values they want to teach their own children by role-modeling healthy relationships.
5. If working in a group, ask for volunteers to share the values that they want to teach their own children. Process participants' answers with a discussion of how a parent might instill that particular value (what kind of role-modeling, etc.)
6. Depending on the level of group intimacy/therapeutic relationship, this activity can also be processed in terms of participants' own experiences growing up in abusive homes. Participant(s) can explore whether they exhibited any of the behaviors listed or learned the lessons violence teaches.
7. After processing the above activities, ask participant(s) to answer the question in the box at the bottom of the page, and share their answers and why or why not with the group or counselor.

Use In Conjunction With:
SEALS III, *"Are You Stuck In the Cycle of Fear?,"* (page 13)
SEALS III, *"Creativity Can Help to Work Through Fear,"* (page 14)
SEALS III, *"Working Through Fear,"* (page 15)
CROSSING THE BRIDGE, (pages 12, 13)

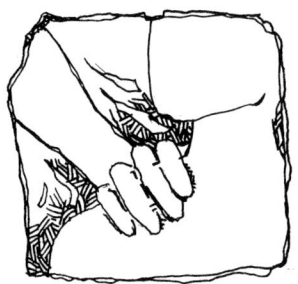

Acquaintance Rape:
What You Can Do To Avoid It!

Most rapes are committed by friends, dating partners or other acquaintances of the victim. Acquaintance rape is any forced, manipulated or coerced sexual contact by someone you know. Here are some strategies for reducing your chances of becoming a victim or perpetrator of date or acquaintance rape.

1. **Communicate clearly.** Decide before you go out with someone how far you want to go with him or her sexually. Do not wait until the 'heat of the moment' to make decisions about sex. Although it can be difficult to talk about sex, use clear, assertive words to convey what you want and don't want. Ask your partners to do the same, and listen and believe them. If either partner communicates in any way that they don't want a particular sexual behavior, respect that. Accept that "no" means "no."

2. **Avoid alcohol and drugs.** They are involved in the majority of rape cases. When drunk or high, people are more vulnerable and less able to make good judgments about their safety. People often use drugs or alcohol as an excuse to get 'out of control.' If you have sex with someone who is too drunk or high to make a good decision, it can be considered rape.

3. **Be aware of your surroundings.** Sexual assault most often occurs in the home or car of one of the people involved. Meet your dates in public places, don't allow yourself to be isolated, and have your own transportation.

4. **Be aware that non-verbal actions may send mixed messages.** No one ever asks to be raped, and rape is never the victim's fault. Unfortunately, however, sometimes people think that a person is "asking for it" by the way they dress, dance, or behave, so it's important to be aware of the way your behavior is seen by others. Sometimes people take flirting or kissing as a message that a person wants sex, no matter what they say. Do not ever make assumptions about what another person wants - ask for clarification.

5. **Make a plan for prevention with your friends.** Talk about what you would do in different dangerous situations so you are prepared. Go out together, look out for each other, and make sure you leave together.

6. **Trust your intuition.** If you feel afraid, say so, and get out of the situation. Don't worry about being polite, looking stupid or hurting someone's feelings.

7. **Use peer pressure to stop abuse.** Let abusive peers know it's not okay. Speak up when friends make sexist jokes, sexually harass others or brag about 'scoring,' because these things show attitudes that can lead to rape. Be a good role model by having respectful relationships. If you witness violence, call the police.

8. **Be aware that nothing you do is a guarantee against sexual assault.** Males and females get raped. If you are assaulted, get help: Call a rape crisis hotline, get medical attention, talk to someone you trust, and remember it's <u>not your fault</u>.

9. _____

10. _____

Facilitator's Information for
Acquaintance Rape: What you Can Do To Avoid It!

Purpose: To develop strategies for reducing the risk of involvement in acquaintance rape.

Materials: One photocopy of worksheet per participant
Pens/pencils
Optional for GROUP: Flipchart and markers/blackboard and chalk

Activity (Group):
1. Begin by reviewing any discussion or activities in past sessions that have focused on sexual abuse. State that today's session will focus on one very common form of sexual abuse, "acquaintance rape" or "date rape."
2. Review the following vocabulary: Acquaintance (anyone you know); Manipulate (trick or talk someone into doing something they don't want to do); Coerce (similar to manipulate, only stronger. To force someone to do something they don't want to do using verbal or non-verbal tactics); Victim (someone who is raped or abused); Perpetrator/Offender (the rapist or abuser.)
3. Review the following definition of Acquaintance Rape: Any time someone is forced, coerced or manipulated into having sex by someone they know.
4. State that while we are using the term rape, which means forced sexual intercourse, this discussion can also apply to any sexual assault that may not necessarily include intercourse.
5. On flipchart or board, write "Things I can do to protect myself from acquaintance rape." Prompt group to brainstorm a list of strategies, and write list on flipchart or board. (During brainstorming, it is likely that participants will engage in victim-blaming; it is important to emphasize that no one is at fault when they are raped and there is no fool-proof way to avoid it, we are just talking about precautions one can take.)
6. Write another heading, "Things I can do to keep myself and friends from raping." Prompt group to brainstorm another list, this time for strategies for making decisions that do not violate others' rights and encouraging friends to do the same.
7. Distribute worksheets and pens/pencils. Read or have participants read aloud the opening paragraph.
8. Read or have participants read each of the strategies for avoiding acquaintance rape, and compare to the group's brainstormed lists. Instruct participants to write any strategies that are not included on the worksheet in the space provided.
9. Split participants into small groups of two to four participants. Assign each group one or two strategies. Give groups five to ten minutes to develop a role-play in which a participant uses the strategy.
10. Before concluding activity, again emphasize with participants that nothing a person can do is a guarantee that they will not be sexually assaulted, and nothing a person does or doesn't do ever makes them to blame if they are raped; the only person responsible for rape is the rapist!!!

Activity (Individual):
1. Begin by reviewing any past sessions that have focused on sexual abuse, and review vocabulary as in #2 above.
2. State that while nobody can guarantee they won't be a victim of rape, there are steps people can take when going out on dates or with friends to try to keep themselves as safe as possible. Engage teen in brainstorming strategies for keeping safe from acquaintance rape.
3. Engage teen in brainstorming another list of strategies for making sure s/he doesn't violate another person's sexual boundaries or rights.
4. Give teen worksheet and read or have teen read introductory paragraph and each strategy, discussing as you go along how each strategy has been used or could be used in a personal situation. Role-play the situations if desired.
5. Suggest teen write in any additional strategies s/he came up with in the space provided.

Follow-up Activities: Let's Talk About Sex (page 83), Practicing Boundary Setting (page 72), Assert Yourself With "I" Statements (page 76)
* Read and discuss chapter titled "Trains" from the book Makes Me Wanna Hollar by NathanMcCall, Vintage Books (1994).

Use In Conjunction With: SEALS+PLUS, "Communication Building Blocks," (page 16)
SEALS II, "Conversation Skills," (page 4)
SEALS III, "Interacting & Coping With Difficult People," (page 32)

How to Help a Friend

If you know someone who's being abused, here's what you can do to help:

1. Be there. Listen without giving advice, unless it is asked for, and believe what he or she tells you.
2. Don't pressure your friend to break up with his or her partner, and don't put the partner down. This may drive your friend away from you when s/he needs you most.
3. Acknowledge your friend's confused feelings. Don't tell your friend how s/he should feel. Recognize that it is still possible to love someone who hurts you.
4. Encourage your friend to get help. Offer to help him or her find a counselor s/he can trust, and offer to go with him or her to meet the counselor.
5. Call a Domestic Violence hotline anonymously to find out what you can do to help your friend.
6. Get written information on relationship abuse and share it with your friend.
7. Don't make victim-blaming statements like "You're stupid to stay with him" or "Why do you let her treat you like this?" This will <u>not</u> help your friend.
8. Don't ever place conditions on support - let your friend know you will support him or her no matter what his or her decisions are.
9. Allow your friend to make his or her own decisions, and respect those decisions even if you don't agree with them.
10. Call the police if you witness physical violence.
11. _____

If you know someone who's abusing a boyfriend or girlfriend, here's what you can do to help:

1. Tell your friend very clearly that his or her behavior isn't cool.
2. Don't laugh at jokes or make light of talk about abusive behavior.
3. If your friend grew up in a violent home, try to get him or her to talk about how that affected his or her own relationships.
4. Encourage your friend to get help. Offer to help him or her find a counselor s/he can trust, and offer to go with him or her to meet the counselor.
5. Be supportive of your friend's partner. Let him or her know s/he doesn't deserve to be abused.
6. Call a Domestic Violence hotline anonymously to find out what you can do to help your friend stop the abusive behavior, and what you can do to help your friend's partner.
7. Get written information on relationship abuse and share it with your friend and your friend's partner.
8. Be a role model for healthy relationships by treating your partner and friends with respect.
9. Speak up when peers make disrespectful remarks or sexist jokes.
10. Call the police if you witness physical violence. In many cases, an abuser can be required to get counseling.
11. _____

Facilitator's Information for
How to Help a Friend

Purpose: To know how to help a peer who is in an abusive relationship.

Materials: One photocopy of worksheet per participant
Additional for GROUP: Flipchart or poster-size paper and markers

Activity (Group):
1. Split group members in half. Give each group a piece of flipchart paper and marker.
2. Assign one group to generate a list of things a person can do when they have a friend who's being abused by a boyfriend or girlfriend. Assign the other group to generate a list of things a person can do when they have a friend who is being abusive to a girlfriend or boyfriend.
3. Allow the groups five or ten minutes to generate lists.
4. Ask each group to post its list. Ask for a volunteer from each group to read and explain the group's strategies. After each group reads its list, ask members of the other group if they have any ideas to add to the list.
5. Distribute worksheets and read or have participants read aloud the strategies for helping a friend and discuss as necessary. If there are any strategies that participants brainstormed that are not included on the worksheet, instruct participants to write them in the space provided.
6. Split group into smaller groups of 2-4 teens.
7. Instruct teens that each group will have five to ten minutes to develop a role-play in which one or more teens are confronting a friend who is in an abusive relationship (either being abused or being abusive.)
8. After teens have developed role-plays, allow each group to perform its role-play for the other group members.
9. Process with the following questions:
   * How realistic do you think the strategies on the worksheet are for teens to follow? Which ones would be more difficult to do?
   * Why is it important not to pressure a person who's being abused to break up with his or her partner?
   * What does 'victim blaming' mean and why can it be so harmful to a person who's being abused?
   * Would it be difficult for a person to confront a friend who's being abusive? What about when other friends are 'going along' with the abusive talk or behavior?
   * What if you knew that repeatedly confronting your friend about his or her abusive behavior would mean you would lose your friend?
   * Could these same strategies apply to a family member or co-worker who's in an abusive relationship?

Activity (Individual):
1. Engage teen in generating a list of strategies for what s/he could do to help a friend who is being abused, and a second list of what s/he could do to help a friend who is being abusive.
2. Give teen worksheet and together review strategies for helping friends in abusive relationships. Discuss as necessary.
3. If teen came up with any strategies that are not included on the worksheet, allow him or her to write in those strategies in the space provided.
4. Suggest a role-play with the counselor playing the part of a friend who's being abused, and the teen playing him or her self trying to help the friend. Next role-play a situation in which the counselor plays the role of an abuser and the teen plays the role of the abuser's friend.
5. Process as in #9 above

Use In Conjunction With:
SEALS+PLUS, *"There ARE Community Resources,"* (page 64)
SEALS II, *"Listening Skills,"* (page 5)
SEALS III, *"HELP,"* (page 79)

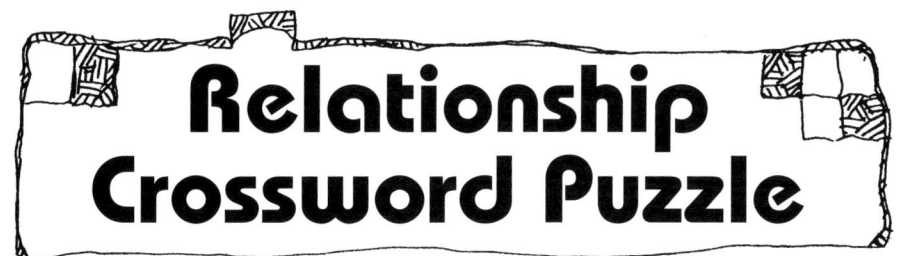

Relationship Crossword Puzzle

How much have you learned about healthy and unhealthy relationships?
Use the clues below and your knowledge of relationship issues to fill in the words in the puzzle.

ACROSS:

1. An abusive relationship is based on one person trying to gain _____ and control over the other.
3. It's like racism, but when a person is discriminated against based on their sex instead of their race.
7. A person who is extremely _____ doesn't trust their partner. This is the number one warning sign of an abusive person.
9. In a healthy relationship both people feel free to _____ their minds, but don't put each other down.
10. A "Power & Control Tactic" when a person cuts his/her partner off from friends, family and activities.
12. Date _____ is when someone you go out with forces you to have sex when you don't want to.
15. When you convince someone to do something they don't want to do, using threats, manipulation, mind games, etc., you _____ them.
16. One example of psychological abuse is playing _____ games.
18. The best way to be sure someone agrees to have sex is to hear them say the word "_____".
19. You can go to court to get an Order of _____, telling your abuser they can't come near you.
20. "No" means "___"!
21. A _____ line is a place you can call 24/7 to get help.
22. Often abusers will tell their partners what to do, what to wear and who to hang out with as a way of _____ them.

DOWN:

1. A person who acts like they own their partner is very _____.
2. A healthy relationship is based on this, when both people have the same amount of value.
4. Put-downs, guilt trips, and humiliating one's partner are examples of this kind of abuse.
5. To act like abuse is "no big deal" is to _____ the abuse.
6. Anyone who is in a violent relationship should develop a written _____ plan.
8. A consequence of unsafe sex (abbreviation).
11. In a healthy relationship, both people can talk and _____ to each other.
13. Using money to control one's partner is called financial or _____ abuse.
14. In a healthy relationship, both people _____ each other's opinion even if they disagree.
16. The stage in the Cycle of Abuse when the abuser is acting loving and kind, is the honey_____ stage.
17. Often abusers will flat-out lie and _____ that the abuse ever happened.
18. There are three parts of a relationship that need to be balanced: Me, _____ and Us.

118

Facilitator's Information for
Relationship Crossword

Purpose: To review terms and concepts associated with healthy and unhealthy relationships.

Materials: One photocopy of worksheet per participant
Pens/pencils

Activity (Group or Individual):
1. Introduce activity as a review of concepts and terms that have been discussed in this workbook.
2. Handout worksheet(s) and pencils.
3. Instruct participant(s) to complete crossword puzzle to the best of their ability. Allow 15-20 minutes to do so.
4. After participant(s) have completed as much of crossword puzzle as possible on their own, go over each clue, giving answers from the answer key only when no participant has been able to figure out the answer. Discuss each concept as you go along.

Answer Key:

	1		2				3	4			5
	P	O	W	E	R		S	E	X	I	S	M
	O		Q			6		S		M		I
	S		U		7	J	E	A	L	O	U	S	8		N
9	S	P	E	A	K			F		T		T		I
	E		L					E		I		D		M
	S		10	I	S	O	L	A	T	I	O	N		I
	S		T			I		Y		N				Z
	I		Y			S			12	R	A	P	E	E
	V				13	E				L				
	E		14	R	15	C	O	E	R	C	E			
			E		O		N					16| M	I	N	D	17
	18		Y	E	S		N					O				E
	O		19	P	R	O	T	E	C	T	I	O	N	20	N	O
	U		E		M							N		Y
			C		I									
21	H	O	T		22	C	O	N	T	R	O	L	L	I	N	G

Use In Conjunction With:
SEALS+PLUS, *"Saying "No","* (page 13)
SEALS II, *"Healthy Relationships,"* (page 42)
SEALS III, *"Evaluate Your Relationship,"* (page 50)
CROSSING THE BRIDGE, (pages 49, 50, 51)

WHERE TO GET HELP AND INFORMATION ON DOMESTIC VIOLENCE

For help and information, call
U.S. National Domestic Violence Hotline
(800) 799-SAFE (TDD: 800-787-3224)
The hotline provides crisis intervention, education, safety planning and referrals
for counseling, shelters and legal services nationwide.

U.S. - For information about domestic violence programs in your area, call your state's domestic violence coalition.

Alabama Coalition Against Domestic Violence
334/832-4842

Alaska Network on Domestic Violence & Sexual Assault
907/586-3650

Arizona Coalition Against Domestic Violence
602/279-2900

Arkansas Coalition Against Violence to Women & Children
501/812-0571

Statewide California Coalition for Battered Women
888-722-2952

Colorado Coalition Against Domestic Violence
303/831-9632

Connecticut Coalition Against Domestic Violence
860/282-7899

Delaware Coalition Against Domestic Violence
302/658-2958

DC Coalition Against Domestic Violence
202/783-5332

Florida Coalition Against Domestic Violence
850/425-2749 - TDD: 800/621-4202

Georgia Coalition on Family Violence
404/209-0280

Hawaii State Coalition Against Domestic Violence
808/486-5072

Idaho Coalition Against Sexual and Domestic Violence
208/384-0419

Illinois Coalition Against Domestic Violence
217/789-2830

Indiana Coalition Against Domestic Violence
317/543-3908

Iowa Coalition Against Domestic Violence
515/244-8028

Kansas Coalition Against Sexual & Domestic Violence
785/232-9784

Kentucky Domestic Violence Association
502/695-2444

Louisiana Coalition Against Domestic Violence
225/752-1296

Maine Coalition for Family Crisis Services
207/941-1194

Maryland Network Against Domestic Violence
301/352-4574

Massachusetts Coalition of Battered Women's Service Groups
617/248-0922

Michigan Coalition Against Domestic Violence
517/347-7000

Minnesota Coalition for Battered Women
651/646-6177

Mississippi Coalition Against Domestic Violence
601/981-9196

Missouri Coalition Against Domestic Violence
573/634-4161

Montana Coalition Against Domestic Violence
406/443-7794

Nebraska Domestic Violence and Sexual Assault Coalition
402/476-6256

Nevada Network Against Domestic Violence
775/828-1115

New Hampshire Coalition Against Domestic and Sexual Violence
603/224-8893

New Jersey Coalition for Battered Women
609/584-8107

New Mexico State Coalition Against Domestic Violence
505/246-9240

New York State Coalition Against Domestic Violence
518/432-4864

North Carolina Coalition Against Domestic Violence
919/956-9124

North Dakota Council on Abused Women's Services
701/255-6240

Ohio Domestic Violence Network
614/784-0023

Oklahoma Coalition on Domestic Violence and Sexual Assault
405/848-1815

Oregon Coalition Against Domestic and Sexual Violence
503/365-9644

Pennsylvania Coalition Against Domestic Violence
717/545-6400

Comision Para Los Asuntos De La Mujer, Puerto Rico
787/722-2907

Rhode Island Council on Domestic Violence
401/467-9940

South Carolina Coalition Against Domestic Violence & Sexual Assault - 803/256-2900

South Dakota Coalition Against Domestic Violence & Sexual Assault - 605/945-0869

Tennessee Task Force Against Family Violence
615/386-9406

Texas Council on Family Violence
512/794-1133

Utah Domestic Violence Advisory Council
801/538-4635

Vermont Network Against Domestic Violence and Sexual Assault
802/223-1302

Virginians Against Domestic Violence
757/221-0990

Washington State Coalition Against Domestic Violence
360/407-0756

West Virginia Coalition Against Domestic Violence
304/965-3552

Wisconsin Coalition Against Domestic Violence
608/255-0539

Wyoming Coalition Against Domestic Violence and Sexual Assault
307/755-5481

Women's Resource Center, Virgin Islands
340/776-3966

Women's Coalition of St. Croix, Virgin Islands
340/773-9272

CANADA
National Clearing House on Domestic Violence
613 957 2938

UNITED KINGDOM
National Domestic Violence Hotline
0345 023 468

ADDITIONAL RESOURCES:
Recommended Readings and Videos

Readings for Professionals on Relationship Abuse and Domestic Violence
- *The Battered Woman.* Lenore E. Walker. Harper & Row, New York, 1979.
- *The Batterer: A Psychological Profile.* Donald G. Dutton and Susan K. Golant. Basic Books, New York, 1995.
- *Boys Will Be Boys: Breaking the Link Between Masculinity and Violence.* M. Miedzian. Anchor Books, New York, NY, 1991.
- *Chain Chain Change, for Black Women Dealing with Physical and Emotional Abuse.* Evelyn C. White. The Seal Press, Seattle, WA, 1985.
- *Confronting Abusive Beliefs.* M.N. Russel. Sage Publications, California, 1995.
- *Dating Violence: Young Women in Danger.* Barrie Levy, ed. The Seal Press, Seattle, WA, 1991.
- *The Domestic Violence Sourcebook.* Dawn Bradley Berry. Lowell House, Los Angeles, 1995.
- *Getting Free: A Handbook for Women in Abusive Relationships.* Ginny NiCarthy. The Seal Press, Seattle, WA, 1985.
- *Helping Teens Stop Violence: A Practical Guide for Counselors, Educators and Parents.* Paul Kivel and Allen Creighton. Hunter House Inc. Publishers, CA, 1994.
- *The Illusion of Love: Why the Battered Woman Returns to Her Abuser.* David P. Celani. Columbia University Press, New York, 1994.
- *Mejor Sola Que Mal Acompanada: For the Latina in an Abusive Relationship* (Spanish & English). Myrna M. Zambrano. The Seal Press, Seattle, WA, 1985.
- *Naming the Violence: Speaking Out Against Lesbian Battering.* Kerry Lagel, ed. The Seal Press, Seattle, WA, 1986.
- *Raising Cain: Protecting the Emotional Life of Boys.* Dan Kindlon and Michael Thompson. Ballantine Books, New York, NY, 2000.
- *Teen Dating Violence Resource Manual.* The National Coalition Against Domestic Violence, Denver, CO, 1997.
- *The Verbally Abusive Relationship: How to Recognize It and How to Respond.* Patricia Evans. Bob Adams, Inc., Holbrook, MA, 1992.
- *What Parents Need to Know About Dating Violence.* Barrie Levy and Patricia O. Giggans. The Seal Press, Seattle, WA, 1995.
- *When Violence Begins at Home: A Comprehensive Guide to Understanding and Ending Domestic Violence.* Karen J Wilson. Hunter House, Alameda, CA, 1997.
- *Sourcebook for Working with Battered Women.* Nancy Kilgore. Volcano Press, CA, 1992.

Readings for Teens
- *Assertion Skills for Young Women.* Ginny NiCarthy. New Directions for Young Women, Seattle, 1981.
- *Coping with Date Violence.* Nancy N. Rue. Rosen Publishing Group, New York, 1989.
- *In Love and in Danger: A Teen's Guide to Breaking Free of Abusive Relationships.* Barrie Levy. The Seal Press, Seattle, WA, 1993.
- *Makes Me Wanna Holler.* Nathan McCall. Vintage Books, New York, 1994.
- *Straight Talk About Date Rape.* Susan Mufson & Rachel Kranz. Facts on File, Inc., New York, 1993.

Suggested Videos for Teens
- *Heart on a Chain: The Truth About Dating Violence.* Coronet/MTI Film & Video, St. Louis, MO (800-777-8100)
- *It Ain't Love.* FACES Theatre Network for Teens, New York, NY (718-283-7861)
- *Rough Love.* National Coalition Against Domestic Violence, Denver, CO (303-839-1852)
- *Twisted Love: Dating Violence Exposed.* In the Mix, New York, NY (212-684-3940)
- *The Vicious Cycle of Domestic Violence.* Yo-TV Production/Educational Video Center, New York, NY (212-725-3534)

REFERENCES

Page i (Foreword)
[1] Jezel, Molidor, and Wright and the National Coalition Against Domestic Violence, *Teen Dating Violence Resource Manual*, NCADV, Denver, CO, 1996.
[2] Berry, Dawn Bradley, *The Domestic Violence Sourcebook,* Lowell House, Los Angeles, 1996.

Page 21 (Myths and Facts)
[1] Levy, B., *Dating Violence: Young Women in Danger*, The Seal Press, Seattle, WA, 1990.
[2] Jezel, Molidor, and Wright and the National Coalition Against Domestic Violence, *Teen Dating Violence Resource Manual*, NCADV, Denver, CO, 1996.
[3] *Uniform Crime Reports*, Federal Bureau of Investigation, 1991.
[4] *Violence Against Women: Estimates from the Redesigned Survey*, U.S. Department of Justice, Bureau of Justice Statistics, August 1995.
[5] Straus, M.A., and Gelles, R.J. (eds), *Physical Violence in American Families*, Transaction Publishers, New Brunswick, NJ, 1990.
[6] Stacy, W. and Schupe, A., *The Family Secret*, Beacon Press, Boston, MA, 1983.
[7] L. Bergman, "Dating violence among high school students," *Social Work* 37(1), 1992.
[8] *Uniform Crime Reports*, Federal Bureau of Investigation, 1991.
[9] Straus, M.A., Gelles, R.J. & Steinmetz, S., *Behind Closed Doors*, Anchor Books, NY, 1980.
[10] Barbara Hart, National Coalition Against Domestic Violence, 1988.
[11] U.S. Department of Justice, Bureau of Justice Statistics' National Crime Victimization Survey, 1995.
[12] U.S. Department of Justice, Bureau of Justice Statistics' National Crime Victimization Survey, 1995.
[13] Berry, Dawn Bradley, *The Domestic Violence Sourcebook*, Lowell House, Los Angeles, 1996.
[14] U.S. Department of Justice, Bureau of Justice Statistics, *Violence by Intimates*, March 1998.
[15] Barnett, Martinez, Keyson, "The relationship between violence, social support, and self-blame in battered women," *Journal of Interpersonal Violence*, 1996.

Page 107 (Is My Relationship Ready for a Baby? Am I?)
[1] Bullock, L. and McFarlane, J., "A program to prevent battering of pregnant students," *Response*, 11 (1), 18-19, 1988.

Page 112 (The Effects of Relationship Abuse on Children)
[1] Fact Sheet, National Coalition Against Domestic Violence, Washington, D.C., 1993.
[2] Jaffe, P. G., Wolfe, D. A. and Wilson, S. K., *Children of Battered Women*, Sage Publications, Newbury Park, CA, 1990.